D1541404

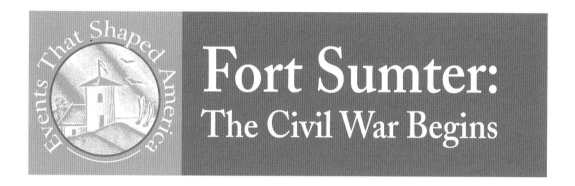

Fort Sumter:
The Civil War Begins

Sabrina Crewe and Michael V. Uschan

Gareth Stevens Publishing

A WORLD ALMANAC EDUCATION GROUP COMPANY

Please visit our web site at: www.garethstevens.com
For a free color catalog describing Gareth Stevens Publishing's list of high-quality
books and multimedia programs, call 1-800-542-2595 (USA) or 1-800-387-3178
(Canada). Gareth Stevens Publishing's fax: (414) 332-3567.

Library of Congress Cataloging-in-Publication Data

Crewe, Sabrina.
    Fort Sumter: the Civil War begins / by Sabrina Crewe and Michael V. Uschan.
      p. cm. — (Events that shaped America)
    Includes bibliographical references and index.
    ISBN 0-8368-3414-3 (lib. bdg.)
    1. Fort Sumter (Charleston, S.C.)—Siege, 1861—Juvenile literature. 2. Charleston
(S.C.)—History—Civil War, 1861-1865—Juvenile literature. 3. United States—
History—Civil War, 1861-1865—Causes—Juvenile literature. I. Uschan, Michael V.,
1948-. II. Title. III. Series.
    E471.1.C93   2005
    973.7'31—dc22   2004058114

This North American edition first published in 2005 by
Gareth Stevens Publishing
A WRC Media Company
330 West Olive Street, Suite 100
Milwaukee, WI 53212 USA

This edition © 2005 by Gareth Stevens Publishing.

Produced by Discovery Books
Editor: Sabrina Crewe
Designer and page production: Sabine Beaupré
Photo researcher: Sabrina Crewe
Maps and diagrams: Stefan Chabluk
Gareth Stevens editorial direction: Mark J. Sachner
Gareth Stevens editor: Monica Rausch
Gareth Stevens art direction: Tammy West
Gareth Stevens production: Jessica Morris

Photo credits: Corbis: cover, pp. 4, 5, 9, 11, 13, 14, 16, (top), 20, 21, 22, 24, 25, 26;
Library of Congress: p. 10; National Park Service/Fort Sumter National Monument:
pp. 23, 27; North Wind Picture Archives: pp. 6, 7, 8, 16 (bottom), 17, 18, 19.

Printed in the United States of America

1 2 3 4 5 6 7 8 9 09 08 07 06 05

Contents

2.14.13

Introduction

An Attack in Charleston Harbor

In 1861, a new fort named Fort Sumter was being built on an island in Charleston Harbor, South Carolina. Although the fort was not finished, a group of U.S. soldiers was inside. By April, they had been there for several months and were running low on supplies.

No ships could bring them food because the fort was surrounded by soldiers of the **Confederate** States of America, also known as the Confederacy. The Confederates had declared their independence from the United States and wanted to take over the fort. The U.S., or **Union**, soldiers inside refused to surrender.

Fort Sumter is still standing in Charleston Harbor. It is now a national monument.

At 4:30 A.M. on April 12, 1861, the Confederates attacked. Cannonballs began raining down on Fort Sumter, and the assault continued for thirty-four hours. The small force inside Fort Sumter fought back bravely but eventually surrendered.

The Civil War

The assault on Fort Sumter began the **Civil War**, a terrible conflict that split the nation into the **North** and **South**. The Confederate states—which included South Carolina and other southern states that no longer wanted to be part of the United States—fought the rest of the United States. The Civil War lasted four years and caused the deaths of hundreds of thousands of soldiers and **civilians**.

The First Shots

"The firing of the [first cannon] woke the echoes from every nook and corner of the harbor, and, in this dead hour of night before dawn, that shot was a sound of alarm that brought every soldier in the harbor to his feet, and every man, woman and child in the city of Charleston from their beds."

Confederate Captain Stephen Lee, who took part in the attack on Fort Sumter

Artillery

The first battle of the Civil War was fought entirely with **artillery,** a name for large guns that can fire ammunition over long distances. The most common

artillery pieces during the Civil War were cannons. A cannon had a large, long barrel mounted on a solid wooden base. Cannons could be loaded with single large balls, multiple pieces of metal, or **shells** that exploded when they landed. Other artillery included howitzers and mortars, both of which were shorter than cannons and fired ammunition at higher angles.

A howitzer on display at Fort Sumter today.

Chapter One

North and South

These looms, used for weaving cotton threads into cloth, were used in the 1800s in Massachusetts.

The North

In the mid-1800s, the United States was mostly a nation of farms and farmers. Things were changing, however. In the 1800s, the first large factories were built and canals and railroads became new forms of transportation. These changes happened mostly in the northeastern states, where factories producing everything from textiles to parts for machinery made the North rich.

In the meantime, new, efficient farm machines appeared that could do the work of many laborers. Over the years, the demand for farm laborers slowly decreased as the need for factory workers grew. Huge numbers of people, therefore, moved to the cities where the factory jobs were.

Comparing the North and the South in 1860

	North	South
Population (figure for the South includes 3.5–4 million slaves)	22,700,000	9,000,000
Percentage of people living in cities and towns	26%	10%
Number of factories	110,000	18,000
Number of industrial workers	1,300,000	110,000
Percentage of cloth manufactured in United States	94%	3%
Percentage of iron produced in United States	93%	7%

Thoroughly Distinct

"There exists a great mistake in supposing that the people of the United States are, or ever have been, one people. On the contrary, never did the sun shine on two people as thoroughly distinct as the people of the North and South."

*Robert Barnwell Rhett, resident of Charleston, South Carolina,
the* New York Tribune, *November 10, 1860*

The South

In the South, the situation was different. The South had fewer railroads and canals, only a handful of large cities, and not many factories. Life was still based around farming, especially growing cotton and tobacco. Huge tobacco and cotton plantations in the South frequently covered thousands of acres (hectares) of land. These plantations depended on large numbers of slaves to provide free labor. The system of slavery, therefore, was very important to white Southerners.

Slaves on plantations in the South were usually given housing and clothing. They received no pay for their work, however, because they were owned, not employed.

Cotton was brought from farms and plantations all over the South to southern ports, such as New Orleans, Louisiana (above). The bales of cotton were then shipped to merchants and cotton mills in the North.

Differences Cause Conflict

Cotton was the United States' major export, and cotton was grown in the South. The cotton trade, however, was controlled by Northerners because shippers, bankers, and merchants were based in the North. Southerners resented the fact that Northerners became rich from cotton produced in the South. Some Northerners, meanwhile, looked down on Southerners because Southerners generally had less education and their agricultural society was "backward."

Victim of Injustice

"What, to the American slave, is your Fourth of July? I answer: a day that reveals to him, more than all other days in the year, the gross injustice and cruelty to which he is the constant victim. To him, your celebration is a sham."

Abolitionist and former slave Frederick Douglass, July 4, 1841

Attitudes to Slavery

Most of all, attitudes and beliefs about slavery caused a sharp divide between the two regions. By the 1800s, slavery had been banned in most northern states, and most people in the North believed slavery should be outlawed altogether. Antislavery campaigners were called **abolitionists**, and for many years they protested the use of slave labor in the South. The protests infuriated white Southerners who believed the South needed slavery to remain strong.

Slavery and Freedom

Men, women, and children who were slaves had no rights. Their owners thought of slaves simply as property, buying and selling them in markets like animals. Slaves could be whipped or killed if they displeased their owners. They worked twelve to sixteen hours a day in the fields and usually had no possessions other than the clothes they wore. If they tried to escape and were caught, slaves would be beaten and sometimes killed. Many thousands of slaves reached freedom, however, often with the help of the Underground Railroad. This transportation system was not a real railroad, but a secret network of hiding places and routes organized to help slaves from the South get to the North. One "railroad" worker, the former slave Harriet Tubman, went south fifteen times to help slaves escape. She took an estimated three hundred people to freedom.

Escaped slaves, helped by Underground Railroad workers, arrive at a safe "station" on their way north.

Fighting about Slavery

The mid-1800s was a time when many white Americans headed west to settle on new lands, and they took their arguments about slavery with them. Southerners wanted slavery to be legal in new **U.S. territories** and states, while Northerners wanted to keep slavery from spreading.

In 1856, proslavery and antislavery groups began openly fighting in Kansas Territory, where both sides had set up their own **legislatures**. The violence was so terrible that the territory became known as "Bleeding Kansas."

HANNIBAL HAMLIN. For Vice President ABRAM LINCOLN. For President

The Republican Party

Meanwhile, a new political group calling itself the Republican Party was gaining support. The Republican Party wanted to abolish slavery in the whole nation. On the other side, the Democratic Party said states and territories should decide slavery issues locally.

The political parties could only gain power if they persuaded the public to elect their candidates. Both sides made speeches to convince people that their party's ideas about running the country were better than the other party's.

The Election of 1860

The Republican candidate for president in 1860 was Abraham

All One Thing or All the Other

"A house divided against itself cannot stand. I believe this government cannot endure, permanently half slave and half free. I do not expect the Union to be dissolved—I do not expect the house to fall—but I do expect it will cease to be divided. It will become all one thing or all the other."

Abraham Lincoln, Lincoln-Douglas debates, Springfield, Illinois, June 16, 1858

THE QUESTION

IF LINCOLN

will be elected or not, is one which interests all parties, North and South. Whether he

IS ELECTED

or not, the people of

SOUTH CAROLINA

(whose rights have been for a number of years trampled upon) have the advantage of supplying themselves with CLOTHING, at the well-known CAROLINA CLOTHING DEPOT, 261 King-street, at such prices as

WILL LEAD

them to be satisfied that the reputation of this Establishment has been

BOLDLY

and fearlessly maintained

FOR A

number of years, supplying its

SOUTHERN

Customers with all the Latest Styles, and at as low prices as any Clothing House *in the present*

CONFEDERACY

of all the States.

Thankful for the liberal patronage extended, the Proprietors desire merely to inform their customers and the public generally, that their present STOCK OF CLOTHING IS COMPLETE in all its departments, and are now prepared to offer Goods on the most reasonable and satisfactory terms. A call is therefore solicited by

OTTOLENGUIS, WILLIS & BARRETT,

November 5   261 King-street.

This advertisement published by the Carolina Clothing Depot in 1860 carries a not-so-hidden message. If you read the small print, it is advertising clothing. The large print spells out a warning against the election of Lincoln.

Lincoln, an Illinois lawyer who had served one term in Congress in the 1840s. In the 1850s, Lincoln won a large following in the North with his speeches against slavery. White Southerners, however, were becoming increasingly fearful that a Republican in the White House would mean the end of slavery and their way of life. They began to talk of **seceding**, or leaving the United States altogether.

On November 6, 1860, Lincoln won the election for president of the United States. Southern leaders, who had threatened they would secede, decided it was time to act.

Chapter Two

Moving toward War

Secession

On December 20, 1860, South Carolina decided to secede from the Union. The reason was simple: South Carolina, one of the states with the highest number of slaves, feared Abraham Lincoln, the new U.S. president, would end slavery.

A headline in the *Charleston Mercury* newspaper the next day boldly proclaimed, "The Union is Dissolved." One observer noted South Carolinians were "wild with excitement" and that the sounds of celebration included "church bells mingling with salvos [shots] of artillery."

This map shows the military sites in Charleston Harbor in 1860 and 1861. It also shows where soldiers of the Confederacy placed their **batteries**, ready to attack Fort Sumter in April 1861.

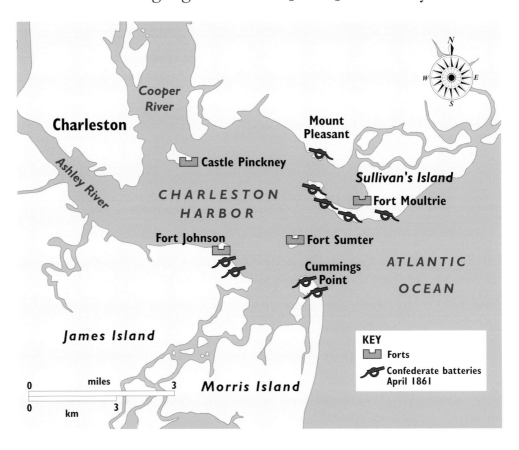

Charleston

Cooper River

Mount Pleasant

Castle Pinckney

Sullivan's Island

Ashley River

Fort Moultrie

CHARLESTON HARBOR

Fort Johnson

Fort Sumter

ATLANTIC OCEAN

Cummings Point

James Island

KEY
⬜ Forts
⚓ Confederate batteries April 1861

miles
0   3
0   3
km

Morris Island

Fort Sumter

Construction of Fort Sumter, named after the American Revolutionary hero General Thomas Sumter, began in 1829. It was located in Charleston Harbor on a small island made from tons of rubble. The fort was massive. Its brick walls towered over 50 feet (15 meters)

Fort Sumter sits on a small island constructed in shallow water in Charleston Harbor.

high and varied in thickness from 12 feet (3.7 m) at the base to 8.5 feet (2.6 m) at the top. Fort Sumter could be armed with 135 large guns, but only a few of them were mounted in position when the attack began in April 1861.

In South Carolina

After secession, the South Carolina government wanted to take over U.S. Army positions in the state and said U.S. soldiers should leave. The U.S. government, however, was not prepared to pull its forces out of the state because that would make it seem as if the United States had accepted South Carolina's act of rebellion.

Charleston, the capital of South Carolina, had four military sites in its harbor: Fort Moultrie on Sullivan's Island, Castle Pinckney on Shute's Folly Island near the city, Fort Johnson on James Island across from Moultrie, and Fort Sumter in the middle of the harbor entrance. Major Robert Anderson, the U.S. Army commander in Charleston Harbor, had been ordered to defend the forts but not to start any conflict. Anderson had only about eighty soldiers to guard the forts. The men were presently stationed at the small, rundown Fort Moultrie.

Moving to Fort Sumter

Fort Sumter was still under construction, but it was the largest and strongest of the forts. Anderson decided to move his men there from Fort Moultrie. On the night of December 26, 1860, Anderson secretly transferred his men to Fort Sumter in rowboats. Also making the trip were forty-five women and children, families of the soldiers.

The next day, South Carolina forces seized Castle Pinckney and Fort Moultrie. Next, on December 30, they took over the U.S. Army's store of weapons in Charleston. Then, on January 2, 1861, they occupied Fort Johnson.

Preparing for Battle

Fort Sumter was now surrounded by South Carolina **militia** in the other forts and on shore. Inside, the Union soldiers began preparing their fort for battle. They readied the cannons and strengthened the building as much as possible.

In January 1861, the U.S. government tried to send two hundred soldiers and supplies to the fort on a private merchant ship, the steamer *Star of the West*. But when the ship arrived in Charleston Harbor on January 9, cannon fire from the shore forced it to turn back.

The night of December 26, 1860, the entire Union force in Charleston moved secretly from Fort Moultrie to Fort Sumter, where it could better defend itself against an attack.

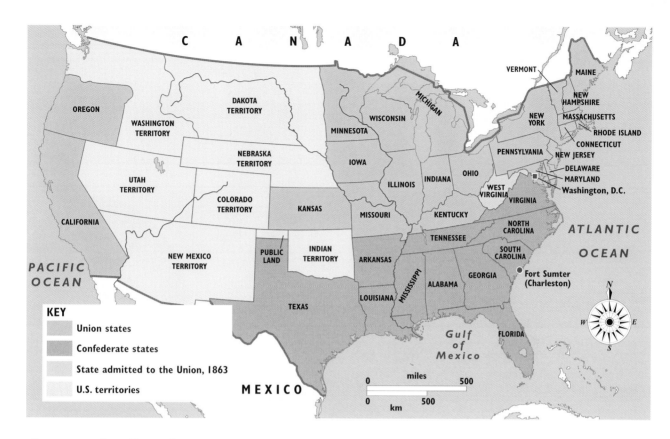

Across the South

In early 1861, Mississippi, Florida, Alabama, Louisiana, Georgia, and Texas announced their secessions. On February 9, 1861, delegates of the seven rebel states met in Montgomery, Alabama, and formed the Confederate States of America. They chose Jefferson Davis from Mississippi as their president.

Lincoln Acts

Meanwhile, Fort Sumter was in trouble. The women and children had been taken back to safety on land, but Anderson's men were running low on supplies.

President Lincoln knew that sending aid to the fort might spark the war he was trying to avoid, but he had to stand up to the military challenge being made by the South. On April 4, 1861, he ordered supply ships to Fort Sumter. When the Confederates learned of Lincoln's decision, Jefferson Davis told the Confederate commander in Charleston, General Pierre Beauregard, to capture Fort Sumter.

This map shows how the states were divided in the early 1860s between those that seceded to join the Confederacy and those that stayed loyal to the Union.

Chapter Three

The Attack

Major Anderson (top) of the Union army was offered a chance to surrender by Confederate commander General Beauregard (bottom). Anderson decided he must try and defend Fort Sumter.

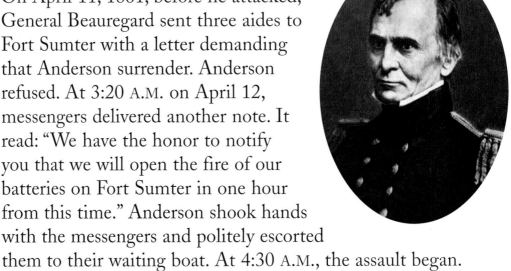

Beauregard Demands Surrender

On April 11, 1861, before he attacked, General Beauregard sent three aides to Fort Sumter with a letter demanding that Anderson surrender. Anderson refused. At 3:20 A.M. on April 12, messengers delivered another note. It read: "We have the honor to notify you that we will open the fire of our batteries on Fort Sumter in one hour from this time." Anderson shook hands with the messengers and politely escorted them to their waiting boat. At 4:30 A.M., the assault began.

First Shots of the Civil War

The first shot exploded harmlessly above Fort Sumter. It was a signal for the bombardment to begin. Within twenty minutes, the artillery pieces around the fort were firing steadily. Confederate soldier D. August Dickert described the continuous firing as "a perfect sheet of flame, a deafening roar, a rumbling, deadening sound." It was all the more dramatic, he said, because it meant "the war was on."

Woken up by the booming blasts, Charleston residents flocked to the harbor to view the attack. To gain a better view of the

Charleston residents watch the attack on Fort Sumter. Some of the spectators feared for the safety of men they knew on either side of the conflict.

action, some people perched on rooftops and climbed church steeples. For them, it was a joyous day—the South was finally standing up to the hated North.

Robert Anderson (1805–1871)

Major Robert Anderson was born near Louisville, Kentucky. After graduating from West Point in 1825, Anderson fought for his country several times, including in the Seminole War of 1837. He taught at West Point Military Academy for several years, and among his students was Pierre Beauregard, who would defeat him at Fort Sumter in 1861. Anderson retired from active service in 1863. In 1869, he went to live in France, where he died two years later.

Watching the Battle

"The living stream poured through all the streets leading to the [harbor] and we found it lined with ranks of eager spectators. There they stood, with palpitating hearts and pallid faces, watching the white smoke as it rose in wreaths and breathing out fervent prayers for their gallant kinsfolk at the guns."

Unidentified Charleston resident and eyewitness of the attack on Fort Sumter, 1861

The Union soldiers in Fort Sumter, seen here in the fort's main battery, began to return fire even though their chances of fending off the attack were small.

A Hopeless Situation

Anderson and his handful of men faced a hopeless situation. They were surrounded by some six thousand Confederate soldiers. They were low on ammunition and other supplies, and they did not know if help would arrive in time. The supply ships ordered by Lincoln on April 4 did finally arrive in Charleston on April 12, but they could not land because the Confederate artillery would have destroyed them.

The men inside Fort Sumter began firing back at Confederate targets, but their counterattack was not very

Pierre Gustave Toutant Beauregard (1818–1893)

Pierre G. T. Beauregard was born in Louisiana and graduated second in his class from West Point Military Academy. On February 20, 1861, Beauregard resigned from the U.S. Army and joined the Confederate army. He would forever be known in the South as the "Hero of Fort Sumter" for winning the first victory of the Civil War. Beauregard went on to lead troops into battle throughout the war. After the war, he was involved in several businesses, including operating a railroad in Louisiana.

strong. They didn't have enough men to fire all the cannons at the same time, and their supply of ammunition was low.

Fire in the Fort

Meanwhile, the Confederates began to heat their shells before firing them. This action made the ammunition hot enough to set structures inside the fort on fire. Fort Sumter filled with thick smoke, and Anderson's small force now had to fight the flames as well as the Confederate soldiers.

Although its walls were immensely strong, heavy shells began tearing away huge chunks of Fort Sumter. The bombardment continued all day April 12 and into the night. Anderson's men stopped firing back in order to conserve their dwindling ammunition. To the surprise of soldiers on both sides, no one had been seriously injured on the first day of battle.

Attacking the Fort

"The effect [of firing] was visible in the impressions made on the walls of Fort Sumter. From our mortar batteries shells were thrown with such precision and rapidity that it soon became impossible for the enemy to employ his guns. . . . The engagement was continued . . . until nightfall, before which time the fire from Sumter had evidently slackened. Operations on our side were sustained throughout the night, provoking, however, only a feeble response."

General Pierre Beauregard, battle report, April 16, 1861

Fort Sumter began to show signs of wear as the attack continued into the night.

The Second Day

As dawn came on April 13, the Confederates intensified their **barrages** of shells and cannonballs. After a breakfast of pork and rice, Union soldiers began to fire back again.

Blazing fires soon became the biggest enemy for the people inside Fort Sumter. By noon, many sections of the fort were on fire, and the defenders feared the flames could ignite stored gunpowder and shells. Although his men were running low on gunpowder, Anderson had them throw several barrels of their precious supply into the sea because fires were closing in.

A Losing Battle

Smoke became so dense in Fort Sumter that soldiers had trouble seeing and breathing. One Union private in the fort later recalled that the "only way to breathe was to lay flat on the ground and keep your face covered with a wet handkerchief."

This drawing, published in a weekly newspaper in April 1861, gives an idea of conditions inside Fort Sumter during the attack.

On shore, the Confederates kept up a relentless bombardment, but they cheered their opponents' determination and bravery.

At 1:00 P.M. on April 13, a shell fragment sent Fort Sumter's flag crashing to the ground. The Confederates thought Anderson had lowered it in surrender, and they stopped firing. When the Union soldiers replaced the flag and began firing again, the Southerners yelled their approval that their enemy was not quitting.

Respect for the Enemy

It was clear all along that the Confederates were winning the battle at Fort Sumter. Even so, they respected their enemy because they knew how brave the Union soldiers were and how difficult it was for them to keep fighting in the smoke and flames that surrounded them. The Confederates even began cheering Anderson's men when they managed to fire back at them. This admiration was part of their southern tradition, a code of honor in which soldiers were taught to respect a brave enemy.

Pandemonium
"The roaring and crackling of the flames, the dense masses of whirling smoke, the bursting of the enemy's shells, and our own which were exploding in the burning rooms, the crashing of the shot, and the sound of masonry falling in every direction, made the fort a pandemonium."

Union captain Abner Doubleday, Reminiscences of Fort Sumter and Fort Moultrie 1860–1861, *1876*

Defending the Fort

"Having defended Fort Sumter for thirty-four hours, until the quarters were entirely burned, the main gates destroyed by fire, the [outer] walls seriously injured, . . . four barrels and three cartridges of powder only being available, and no provisions remaining but pork, I accepted terms of evacuation offered by General Beauregard."

Major Robert Anderson, battle report, April 18, 1861

Surrender

In that brief interlude in which the fighting had stopped, however, a Confederate officer went to offer Anderson a final chance to surrender. Colonel Louis Wigfall rowed to the fort and climbed into the battered fort while holding a white handkerchief as a sign of truce.

Wigfall told the Union commander he had fought bravely but should give up because he could not win. Anderson realized Wigfall was right. "Well, I have done all that was possible to defend this fort," Anderson said. He had the U.S. flag replaced with a white one of surrender. After thirty-four hours of nearly continuous bombardment of Fort Sumter, the first battle of the Civil War had ended with a Confederate victory.

This flag was the first Confederate flag raised over Fort Sumter. It is the Palmetto flag, adopted by South Carolina after the state seceded from the Union.

A Tragic End

The formal surrender took place at 4:00 P.M. on April 14, 1861, and Anderson took the traditional military ceremony seriously. His men marched out "with colors flying and drums beating," he later reported, to the tune of "Yankee Doodle." Anderson ordered his men to fire fifty guns while the U.S. flag was being lowered for the last time.

When the forty-seventh gun was fired, a spark accidentally ignited some gunpowder. The resulting explosion killed Union privates Daniel Hough and Edward Galloway and injured four other soldiers. It was a tragic end to a battle that had been nearly without bloodshed.

After marching out of the fort they had so bravely defended, Anderson and his men were put on a Confederate vessel that transferred them to a Union ship waiting off the coast. The soldiers sailed to New York City, where they were welcomed as heroes.

This photo shows Fort Sumter soon after the Union troops surrendered. The "Stars and Bars" flag flying overhead was the first national Confederate flag.

Chapter Four

The Civil War

The Civil War Begins

When President Lincoln learned of the attack on Fort Sumter, he ordered state militias in the North to raise a combined army of 75,000 men to put down the rebellion by southern states. The Union had a huge advantage over the South, with more men, more wealth, and the factories to produce guns and other weapons.

The Confederates were determined to fight, however. Four days after Fort Sumter fell, Virginia became the eighth state to secede. During May 1861, Arkansas, Tennessee, and North Carolina also joined the Confederacy.

A Long War

Both the North and South had high hopes of winning, but the war would not be won easily. The battles of the Civil War continued for years, shattering families and destroying land and buildings. In one single day—September 17, 1862—the Battle of Antietam in Maryland resulted in over 26,000 **casualties**.

Union artillery destroyed much of Charleston and other southern cities during the Civil War. This photograph shows ruins in Charleston at the end of the war in 1865.

A New Cause

On January 1, 1863, in the midst of war, President Lincoln issued the **Emancipation** Proclamation, which declared that all slaves in the Confederacy were free. Although the proclamation was ignored in the South, it served an important purpose in the Union. Lincoln knew that as the war dragged on, Northerners needed an additional cause for which to fight. Not only would they fight to save the Union, but they would also fight to free the slaves.

The North Triumphs

The tide soon began to turn against the South. The biggest blow came on July 1 to 3, 1863, when the Union defeated the Confederate army in Pennsylvania at the Battle of Gettysburg. In the next two years, the Union's advantages in men and weaponry began to wear down the Confederacy. On April 9, 1865, Confederate General Robert E. Lee surrendered to the Union in Virginia.

General Lee surrendered to the Union's General Ulysses S. Grant at Appomattox Court House in Virginia. This drawing shows the surrender, with Lee (seated center left) and Grant (seated center right) surrounded by other soldiers.

Conclusion

Fort Sumter during the Civil War

Before the Civil War was over, Confederates successfully defended Fort Sumter against several Union attacks. Its strong, towering walls, however, were reduced to mostly rubble by a twenty-two-month **siege** that began in April 1863. During the siege, Union ships pounded Fort Sumter with artillery. Despite the tremendous assault, the Confederates did not surrender. They finally had to leave on February 17, 1865, as Union troops advanced on the fort.

Return to Fort Sumter

When Major Robert Anderson left Fort Sumter in defeat on April 14, 1861, he took with him one of the flags that had flown above the fort during the 1861 attack. On April 14, 1865, Anderson returned with the scorched and tattered U.S. flag. He hoisted it up a pole to fly over the fort. "I thank God

Confederate forces on the shore try to fight off a Union fleet intent on attacking Fort Sumter in April 1863. The Confederates inside Fort Sumter held out against the siege for nearly two years.

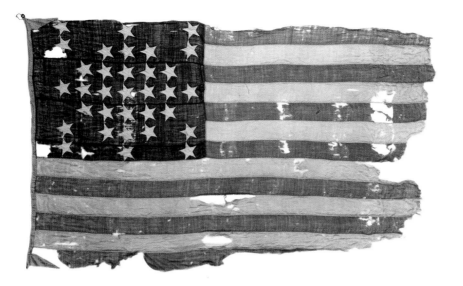

After the large flag flying over Fort Sumter was brought down on April 13, 1861, Union soldiers raised this smaller flag in its place. It is now on display at Fort Sumter for visitors to see.

that I have lived to see this day," said Anderson. Coming only five days after the South surrendered, the flag ceremony at Fort Sumter was intended as a symbolic end to the Civil War.

A National Monument

After the Civil War, Fort Sumter was partially rebuilt. In the decades that followed, it was occasionally used as a lighthouse. It was manned during the Spanish-American War, World War I, and World War II as a lookout for enemy ships. In 1948, Fort Sumter became a national monument. Much of the original fort is still in ruins, preserved for visitors to see it as it was during the Civil War.

The Human Cost of the Civil War

Because there are no exact records, historians can only guess how many Union and Confederate soldiers died in the Civil War. The most accepted estimate is that more than 650,000 Americans died—about 380,000 Northerners and 270,000 Southerners. However, some historians believe the death toll may have been as high as 700,000. That number does not include civilians who died during fighting that took place in or near their communities. In addition, hundreds of thousands of soldiers were wounded, many of them affected for the rest of their lives by the loss of limbs or other horrific injuries.

Time Line

1860   November 6: Abraham Lincoln is elected president.
December 20: South Carolina secedes from the Union.
December 26: Union force in Charleston moves to Fort Sumter.
December 27–30: South Carolina militia seize Fort Pinckney, Fort Moultrie, and U.S. Army's store of weapons in Charleston.

1861   January 2: South Carolina militia seize Fort Johnson.
January 9: The *Star of the West* is turned back when it tries to enter Charleston Harbor.
January 9–February 1: Mississippi, Florida, Alabama, Georgia, Louisiana, and Texas secede from the Union.
February 9: Confederate States of America is formed.
April 4: President Lincoln orders supply ships to Fort Sumter.
April 11: Confederate general Pierre Beauregard demands Union surrender of Fort Sumter; Major Robert Anderson refuses.
April 12: Confederates begin attack on Fort Sumter.
April 13: Major Anderson surrenders Fort Sumter to Confederates.
April 14: Surrender ceremony at Fort Sumter.
April 17: Virginia secedes from the Union.
May: Arkansas, Tennessee, and North Carolina secede from the Union.

1862   September 17: Battle of Antietam.

1863   January 1: Lincoln issues the Emancipation Proclamation.
July 1–3: Battle of Gettysburg.

1865   February 17: Confederates evacuate Fort Sumter after twenty-two-month Union siege.
April 9: Confederate surrender ends Civil War.
April 14: U.S. flag is ceremoniously raised over Fort Sumter.

Things to Think About and Do

Confederate and Union Soldiers

Write an account of the attack on Fort Sumter from the point of view of a Union soldier inside the fort. Then write another account of the attack, this time from a Confederate soldier's point of view. You can describe the actual events and how it felt to be there, and you can also explain what causes you were fighting for and why they were important to you.

The Underground Railroad

Find out more about the Underground Railroad and how it operated. Imagine you are a slave from the South escaping to the North with the help of the Underground Railroad, and write a journal of your experience.

Glossary

abolitionist: person who supports or works toward ending slavery.

artillery: large, heavy guns such as cannons.

barrage: rapid firing of lots of artillery.

battery: artillery unit that, during the Civil War, usually included four to eight guns.

casualty: person who is wounded, killed, or missing in battle.

civil war: war between groups of people in the same nation.

civilian: person who is not a member of the armed forces.

confederate: joined together in a common cause, such as the states that formed the Confederate States of America.

emancipation: freeing of enslaved African Americans.

legislature: group of officials that makes laws.

militia: group of citizens organized into an unofficial army (as opposed to an army of professional soldiers).

North: northern states of the United States; and the remaining United States during the Civil War after the other states seceded.

secede: withdraw from the Union.

shell: case that contains explosives and is fired from a gun.

siege: military operation in which a group of attackers surrounds a target and either attacks it or keeps it trapped in order to force a surrender.

South: southern states of the United States; and the states that seceded and formed the Confederacy during the Civil War.

Union: United States of America under a single government. "Union" is the term used to describe the remaining United States during the Civil War after the other states seceded.

U.S. territory: geographical area that belongs to and is governed by the United States but is not included in any of its states.

Further Information

Books

Herbert, Janis. *The Civil War for Kids: A History with 21 Activities.* Chicago Review Press, 1999.

January, Brendan. *Fort Sumter* (Cornerstones of Freedom). Children's Press, 1998.

Murphy, Jim. *The Boys' War: Confederate and Union Soldiers Talk about the Civil War.* Clarion, 1993.

Riehecky, Janet. *The Emancipation Proclamation: The Abolition of Slavery* (Point of Impact). Heinemann, 2002.

Stanchak, John E. *Eyewitness: Civil War.* Dorling Kindersley, 2000.

Web Sites

www.civilwarhome.com/ftsumter.htm First-person accounts and military histories of the attack on Fort Sumter.

www.cr.nps.gov/history/online_books/hh/12/hh12toc.htm Online version of illustrated National Park Service historical handbook about Fort Sumter.

www.nationalgeographic.com/features/99/railroad/index.html Web site offering interactive journeys on the Underground Railroad and follow-up activities.

www.nps.gov/fosu Information and images from the National Park Service to do with the Fort Sumter National Monument, which includes Fort Moultrie.

Useful Addresses

Fort Sumter National Monument
National Park Service
1214 Middle Street
Sullivan's Island, SC 29482
Telephone: (843) 883-3123

Index

The Sitting & Talking Place

The Story of a Man and his Grandson

Dr. Jerry Edward McGee

Deacon Press
Charlotte, North Carolina

The Sitting & Talking Place: The Story of a Man and His Grandson

Published by: Deacon Press, Charlotte, North Carolina

Library of Congress Catalog Number: Applied for

ISBN 0-966-1201-8-3

Book and Jacket Design: Steve Thomas - Set?Communicate!

Address all inquiries to:
Dr. Jerry E. McGee
P.O. Box 3105
Wingate, North Carolina 28174
Phone: (704) 233-8111
email: mcgee@wingate.edu

Dedication

This work is dedicated
to the memory of
Hannah Covington McGee
in appreciation for a lifetime of
love and devotion.

Foreword

I undertook this project for several reasons. First, I wanted my two sons, Ryan and Sam, to have this glimpse of our family history. Ryan was three years old and Sam two months old when Granddaddy McKinnon died, so they know very little about the man who played such a vital role in my life. I hope they will now know him and our other family members a little better and can have a greater appreciation of the sacrifices made on our behalf.

Secondly, I wrote on behalf of thousands of other people who have had their lives blessed by a special relationship with a grandparent but have never been able to share the memories with others. I hope my attempt will encourage them to undertake similar efforts to honor their grandparents and other relatives. If they do, I am sure they will enjoy visiting with their long departed loved ones as much as I did.

Introduction

Several years after my Granddad's death, my wife Hannah and I made our first trip to England and Scotland with friends. As we traveled by train from London to Edinburgh, I began talking about my family's Scottish heritage. As we passed through the lush green rolling hillsides, we would occasionally see a sheep rancher walking or sitting alone beside his herd of sheep. I would turn to the others and say with absolute certainty, "It's a shame my ancestors ever came to America. My Granddad would have been so much happier sitting in a beautiful meadow with only his sheep to communicate with . . . or maybe just the sheep and his grandson." I thought of my Granddad's love for animals and how he loved the soil and enjoyed sitting on a creek bank with a fishing pole in his hand, whether the fish were biting or not. It wasn't that he didn't like people. He just loved the peace and tranquility that clanging textile machinery and busy mill villages simply didn't allow. There was no question, Granddad would have been much happier in a quiet little farm borough in Scotland than in East Rockingham, North Carolina. Then it struck me that I could write about this special man and the relationship we shared. However, the twin urgencies of an aspiring career and a family that rightfully demanded much of my time caused me to set aside this idea for a later time.

The deaths of both my Mama and Daddy over the past several years have changed me in many ways, some positive and perhaps some not so positive. I surely have been more reflective on my life — a life which has been blessed beyond description. I have also been better able to appreciate the positive influence so many people have had on me, hopefully resulting in me being a better person, neighbor, friend, husband and father. While acknowledging the meaningful investments that many have made in my life, I continue to think first of my Granddad, Willie Clarence

McKinnon. Again, the deaths of my parents have made me more dedicated to acknowledging the contributions of my family to any success that we or our children might enjoy. I have yearned for a small slice of life which I could dedicate to writing about Granddad and hoped that my planned three month sabbatical from my work at Wingate University would provide it.

The first few days of our leave were dedicated to rest and relaxation. Then we took a few days to familiarize ourselves with the tiny village of Cane Garden Bay on the Island of Tortola in the British Virgin Islands, which we had chosen for our retreat. Then late one evening Hannah and I were sitting on the veranda of our villa, overlooking the bay filled with sailboats. I had just made a casual reference to my Granddad's Scottish heritage when someone on one of the sailboats stood and played, "Amazing Grace" on his bagpipes. I smiled at Hannah, picked up a pencil, and began writing.

Table of contents

Mary and her baby

For a life that's had so many wonderful blessings, mine didn't get off to such a great start. In a two room duplex on the tiny unpaved Seaboard Street on the Hannah Pickett Mill Village, near Rockingham in the Sandhills section of North Carolina, a pretty young woman was experiencing the best and the worst life had to offer. My mother, Mary McKinnon, had married Sam McGee a year earlier. Many people had questioned her judgement for marrying someone 13 years older than she, but she was simply following her heart. Now when the family doctor, Dr. Zachary Long, made a house call, he was helping her through a difficult pregnancy and caring for her husband, who was critically ill. It was important to her that her beloved Sam McGee had the opportunity to see his child before his death. She got her wish.

I was born on November 4 and she and Sam decided to name me Jerry. Three months later, Sam McGee, ravaged by Bright's Disease, died. So now Mary, all of 20 years of age, was a widow with a child in a country recovering from the Great Depression and engaged in World War II. Just a couple of blocks away, Mary's parents, Will and Betty McKinnon, were raising their remaining children — Archie, Hayden, Don, twin daughters Loyce and Joyce, and Bobby, who was barely three years old.

Several things happened during the next few months which demonstrated the genuine goodness of mankind. First, the mill leadership ignored its strict rule making people move immediately when no one in the family was working in the mill. They based their decision on two things — Mary McKinnon McGee wasn't physically or emotionally able to work or move; furthermore, her father, Will McKinnon, was a highly respected worker in the plant. Besides, he had six other children who would also probably wind up working in the mill. If they proved to be hard working, dedicated employees like Will, the patience of the company would be rewarded.

Like Mary, Sam McGee had come from a family known for its honesty and strong family ties. His brother, Will McGee, in his sweet and gentle way, made his way to visit Mary to offer a well thought out solution to her problem. He told her that he appreciated the way she loved his brother and especially the fact that she had presented him with a fine son. He spoke of Mary's youth and beauty and how difficult it would make her life, trying to work and provide for a little boy.

The Sitting & Talking Place

His solution was direct and appealing. He and his wife, Claudia, lived on a farm eight miles or so south of Rockingham, not too far from the South Carolina - North Carolina border. They had several children of their own and they offered to take me, little Jerry, into their family and raise me with the other McGee children. Will promised to provide a home full of love and values she would be proud of. He also mentioned that a boy raised on the farm wouldn't face the dangers that were always present in the mill villages.

My Mama's response was just as direct. She had loved Sam McGee with all of her heart, and the last thing she could do for him was to raise his son. She understood how sincere Will and Claudia were in their generous offer, but declined it just as graciously as it had been offered.

Granddad and Ma McKinnon also had a solution for Mama's consideration. With eight people already living in the four room house they occupied, two more wouldn't make much difference. After Mama was ready, she would go to work and Ma could watch after me. I could grow up with their little Bobby. Mama finally agreed after being convinced that Archie would soon be going to work himself and getting a place of his own. It was also understood that Mama would help Ma with household chores and pay her own way as she was able. I have no idea where everybody slept, but families have a way of working those things out.

Thus began a relationship with grandparents which proved to be more important than any of us could imagine. I was never quite sure whether they considered me to be their oldest grandchild or their youngest son. But, I'm sure that much of what they did for me and the way they loved me was designed to show me that even though my daddy had died, I would never be alone.

It all seemed like a lot of fuss about one skinny little black haired boy.

 The Sitting & Talking Place

Bye-bye, kitty!

Mama and I lived with her family for the first 4 years of my life. It was great having so many people looking after me. I felt especially close to Uncle Bobby, because he was only three years older than me, and Uncle Don, because he would take me to the motion picture theater located between the Aleo and Hannah Pickett villages. All the rest of the aunts and uncles dutifully took their turns looking after me, but couldn't wait to turn me over to Mama when she got home.

Most of my time was spent following Ma or Granddad around the house and yard. It seemed like we always had a dog and a cat around the house, along with a few chickens. The animals generally ate table scraps when Ma had a few left after feeding our army. I remember Granddad always fussing about "all these dad-blame animals that don't do anything but eat, sleep and get in my way."

Suddenly, one day the old cat started acting a little funny and actually became quite a grump. She didn't want to be petted and started swatting the old dog around like a punching bag. Granddad didn't act too surprised and reminded us menfolks that we were dealing with a woman cat, and they could be just as strange as real women. A few days later we all got a real surprise — four kittens. We spent all morning watching the old mama cat care for her kittens, being careful not to get too close. When the two o'clock whistle blew, we ran towards the mill to share the exciting news with Granddad. It was safe to say that he was neither surprised, nor particularly excited, about this news. Because of our urging, he went with us to see the new additions. He just shook his head and told us we could keep the kittens for a few weeks, but as soon as "they don't need their mama any longer, we need to give each one to a neighbor." That suited us, but we had no idea that the moms and dads in the Hannah Pickett village would be just about as excited about kittens as Granddad was. We finally got our cousins around the corner to take one, and Granddad reminded us everyday that we needed to "find a new home for the rest of the little varmints."

I was always around Ma and Granddad while the other kids played in the neighborhood, so I overheard them discussing the kittens. They were concerned that there would not be enough table scraps to feed these new residents. Granddad made a comment about "getting rid of them one way or the other." That night I couldn't sleep as I thought about those poor kittens and what we could do with them. I wasn't sure what Granddaddy had meant earlier, but I didn't like the sound of it. I figured "get rid of them" meant throwing them in the trash can or something as bad.

Granddad was a respected worker in the mill. He never missed a day, always worked overtime when needed and didn't cause any fuss. Therefore, he had one of the nicest houses, though not the biggest, in the village. In fact, while most workers lived in mill-owned houses with outdoor toilets, our house had a toilet in a little room on the back porch. With so many people living in our house (nine, once Archie moved out), you almost had to make an appointment to use the toilet. I usually took my turn after dinner, our mid-day meal, while the other kids were at school and Granddad was working. One day when I found the toilet unoccupied, I took the remaining three kittens and went inside. After carefully latching the door, I put the first kitten in the toilet, pulled the chain and gave it a flush. Then I repeated this act of kindness two more times. I didn't know where they might be going, but, in my three year old mind, I knew it was better than being thrown in the trash can and hauled away.

My plan failed because as Mama was getting ready for work, she heard me say "bye - bye, kitty" as I flushed each one away. She knocked the door latch loose and proceeded to save all three kittens from drowning by reaching down in the commode and pulling them out one by one. They were kind of strange looking when they were dry, but they were really ugly when they were soaked. I didn't want anything else to do with them. Needless to say, they didn't understand that I was trying to help them, and they stayed away from me and the toilet for quite a while.

As usual, Granddad had the last word. After he heard what I had tried to do, he chuckled a little and said, "Sounds like the boy had a pretty good idea. Why'd you stop him?" Granddad was softer than he ever wanted any of us to know. He never got rid of the kittens.

The Sitting & Talking Place

A new daddy

Just when you're beginning to understand life, something happens to confuse you and make you start over. Mama and I were becoming comfortable living with Ma, Granddad and her brothers and sisters (as comfortable as you can be with nine people living in a four room house), when along came Robert Marshall Caddell. Over the years he told me many times about returning from service in the U. S. Army during World War II and going to work at Safie Mill. It was there that he met my mother. After weeks of observing her beauty from a distance, he somehow arranged an introduction and asked her out. He must have really been smitten, because he seemed not to care that she had a little boy from a previous marriage.

After a few months courtship, he got Granddad's permission and asked Mary McKinnon McGee to marry him. Stories are told frequently about stepparents who never love their stepchildren, but that was not the case with Robert Marshall Caddell. From the day he married my mother until the day he died, he loved me with all of his heart and proved it over and over during our fifty years together.

It's easy for a stepfather to decide what to call his stepson — you simply call him by his name — Jerry. However, a whole new set of problems arise when a stepson has to decide what to call a stepfather. When faced with this situation, I did what I always seemed to do when searching for an answer. I asked my Granddad.

One thing I loved about my Granddad was that when we talked, he always listened like he was really interested. He asked how I liked my new stepdaddy. I told him that he was nice and I liked him a lot, but I explained that I didn't know what to call him. Granddad seemed to understand and asked me what other people called him. I told him some people called him Robert and others called him Marshall. He then asked if that's what I wanted to call him. I quickly answered, "NO!" He told me that he was sure my stepdaddy would be happy no matter what I called him. He asked, "What do you want to call him?" I told him that all my friends had their real dads and that all of them just called them "daddy." Since my daddy was dead, I wondered if it would be okay for me to call my stepfather "daddy." Granddad put his arms around me and said "Geeboy (the nickname given to me by my Granddad), I think Robert Marshall Caddell would be mighty happy if you called him 'daddy'."

So the next day when Robert Marshall Caddell and I were on our way home from getting a haircut, I told him all my friends had real "daddies" and I wanted to know if I could call him "daddy." He nodded his head and said "Of course. That's exactly what I want you to call me. Would it be okay for me to call you my son?" My grin surely gave away my answer. "Sure . . . daddy."

Neither Granddad or I had any idea how happy that short conversation would make Robert Marshall Caddell, but over the years there were dozens of times when we would pass the spot where it happened. He would always slow down and tell me the story one more time. In fact, the final time we went to dinner together, just a few days before his unexpected death in 1998, he reminded me one last time of the day a little boy changed his life by asking permission to call him "daddy."

Thank you, Mama, for picking exactly the right stepfather for me. Thank you, Granddad, for giving me the courage to call him "daddy."

The Sitting & Talking Place

The Safie strike

There were quite a few textile operations in Richmond County in the 1950's; however, most textile employees agreed that the best company to work for was Safie Manufacturing Company. The houses in the Safie village were well maintained by the company. Safie also had a very nice company store and a movie theater for its employees. Their outstanding baseball team played at a beautiful ball park and provided a terrific rallying point for the community. Quite a few successful small businesses surrounded the mill, making the two mile trip to Rockingham an infrequent necessity. If the husband and wife worked in different departments in the plant, their supervisors would allow one to leave his or her department so they could enjoy meals together. Most importantly, the company paid well and didn't try to enforce unrealistic production requirements. If you were a textile family, you were mighty lucky to work at Safie.

Still, it seems some people are never quite satisfied. Some of the Safie workers, aided by outside agitators, started making requests for unreasonable pay, working hours and conditions. They even tried to organize a union. Of course, a majority of employees were happy and didn't support the union movement so a call for a work stoppage or "strike" against the company failed. However, some of the unhappy workers still refused to show up for work, causing production problems. Everyone in our family kept working and agreed to work overtime if necessary to keep the plant operating. This decision put them at odds with the more rebellious workers and created a situation that proved to be confrontational and dangerous.

Our family had developed a routine allowing our married family members to be on the same shift. As you can imagine, it was very difficult when one spouse worked from 2 PM to 10 PM and the other spouse worked from 6 AM to 2 PM or 10 PM till 6 AM. Working different shifts allowed very little family time and often put a lot of strain on marriages. Rather than depending on professional daycare, families and neighbors worked together to provide care for the children. Granddad worked from 6 AM to 2 PM and Ma didn't work outside the house. Mama and Daddy would drop me off at my grandparents' house about 1:30 PM and report to work at 2 PM. I would spend the afternoon and evening with my grandparents. At 9:30 PM I would ride to the plant with one of my uncles who worked from 10 PM to 6 AM. He would park his car as close as possible to Mama and Daddy's car. When they got off work at 10 PM, they were at their car in just a few moments and they would pick me up and we would go home together. I loved that arrangement because I got to spend a lot of time with Uncle Bobby, my aunts Loyce and Joyce, and my grandparents. Often my parents and I would stop on the way home and get a sandwich or an ice cream cone, which I also didn't mind.

One night when the tension between those who wanted to work and those who wanted to strike was at its highest, a car filled with four strikers followed us home, shining their bright lights on us all the way. They actually turned into our driveway and sat in their car yelling obscenities at my parents. Marshall Caddell, my stepfather, had been a decorated serviceman in World War II and was quite a physical specimen. He stood about 5 feet 9 inches tall and weighed about 220, with huge arms and legs. He told Mama to stay in the car and to watch after me. He said, "I need to speak to those fellows a minute." He walked back to the car and quietly spoke to the men. The driver obviously said something that he shouldn't have because Daddy reached in the window, pulled him about halfway out and slapped him in the face six or eight times. He then said in a rather loud voice, "If you want to deal with me man to man, it's okay by me. If you ever threaten my family again, you'll regret it." The car sped away, and we were never bothered again.

Unfortunately, this story has a sad ending. After continued bitterness between the absentee ownership of Safie Manufacturing Company and the unhappy minority of workers, the mill closed. This was devastating news for the economy of Richmond County and for many families and small businesses. No family suffered more than ours. Granddad, Mama, Daddy, Uncle Archie, Uncle Don and Uncle Hayden and his wife, Daisy, all were employed by Safie and all were faced with mortgages, car payments and growing families. Granddad quickly gathered the family together and told everybody not to panic. Everyone would be receiving unemployment compensation for a while and nobody should feel bad about accepting this assistance. It was well earned and the company certainly owed them. He said, "I know a lot

 The Sitting & Talking Place

of people will be looking for jobs, but our family is known for its honesty, hard work and loyalty to our employers. We all might have to take a job we don't particularly like, or drive a little ways for a while, but we will all come out of this okay. Betty and I have a little money saved. Let us know if you need our help." He then talked to each couple, or individual, privately about their skills and work experience and about where they would prefer to work.

These were traumatic times but Granddad McKinnon was right on target. By sticking together, all of his family members had good jobs within a few months. Unfortunately, Richmond County's economy seems to have never recovered from the close of the Safie Manufacturing Company nearly a half century ago.

The Sitting & Talking Place

My other grandfather

Little boys hear a lot better than most adults realize. Just because you're coloring or playing marbles or talking to other kids, doesn't mean you can't hear adult conversations. Either Jule Caddell, my stepfather's father, didn't know I could hear or he didn't mind bruising my feelings a little every now and then. Sometimes he made hurtful comments about me to others when I was close enough to hear. And, occasionally, he looked right at me and purposefully said mean things. Either way, they hurt just the same. I never could quite figure out why he thought my Mama and I were not good enough for him. Heaven knows, his wife, Vonnie Caddell, was a saint because she put up with his sour personality and still loved everybody she came in contact with. I can still smell her sugar cookies as they came out of the oven, soon to be gobbled up by her grandchildren, and later, her great-grandchildren. Regrettably, I let my dislike of her husband keep me from remaining close to her even after he was gone. I'm sad about that.

Most of my childhood memories are happy ones. Although we didn't have much in terms of material possessions, we had everything we needed — clean clothes, a warm house, food to eat, pets to love and a close family. Almost all of my unhappy memories are of a few neighborhood bullies and a handful of unpleasant adults I encountered along life's way. Absolutely, the most unpleasant adult I had to deal with was Jule Caddell. He moved around a lot, I guess because he was never quite satisfied with himself or his life. He obviously thought he was too good to work in the mills so he always seemed to have a little store to run. Having a step-grandparent who owned a store should have been a good thing, but Jule Caddell never let anything remain pleasant very long. As I recall, some of our most unpleasant exchanges took place in one of his little stores.

Mama, Daddy and I lived in the village of Roberdel, about four miles north of Rockingham, just a 10 minute drive from the Safie community. At one time Roberdel had three churches — Baptist, Methodist and Presbyterian. After years of struggles, the Presbyterian church closed and Jule and Vonnie Caddell moved into the back of the building and opened a store in the front. As I remember, it wasn't much of a store, but it had bread, soft drinks, candy, milk, cookies, a few canned goods and some household items. It was there that I began to see quite a difference in the way Jule Caddell treated his other grandchildren and the way he treated me.

The differences were sometimes obvious to others, sometimes not, but they were always obvious to me, and they broke my heart more than once. One Saturday afternoon, the grandsons and I were playing out back when Grandmother Caddell called us in for a lunch of bologna sandwiches. After she saw to it that our hands were washed, she told us to go out front to the store and get one cookie each out of the big jar on the counter. This would be our dessert. We were thrilled because although the cookies cost only 1 cent each, they were really big and delicious as well. Jule Caddell held the jar as each boy reached in to get the cookie that suited his taste. I was last in line. As I was pulling my cookie from the jar, Jule Caddell jerked the jar away quickly, partly to let me know he resented me having a free cookie and partly to amuse a couple of men who had dropped into the store for a soft drink. His unexpected move made me drop the cookie on the counter and it broke into several pieces. I quickly grabbed them up and then hurried to the safety of Grandmother's kitchen. As I ran away, I heard Jule Caddell's stinging comment to his customers, "You can't make nothing out of mill hill trash."

Out under the big oak trees beside the store was the favorite "hanging out" spot for the young men in the Roberdel neighborhood. They would drink 12 ounce soft drinks, and either leave the empty bottles lying around or throw them into the woods. Jule Caddell often fussed about, "each one of them bottles cost me 1 cent deposit. I wish those kids would bring them back into the store." At some point I just started going out and picking up bottles and bringing them inside in an attempt to help old hateful Jule Caddell a little bit. He never thanked me once, but Grandmother Caddell did. In her sweet, gentle way she even talked him into a deal where he would pay me 1 cent for each bottle I retrieved from the woods. He reluctantly gave his approval and for the first time in my life, I was going to be paid based on production, sort of like Mama and Daddy were paid at the mill. So the next time I visited the store, I went outside and gathered up all the bottles left near the store building. I brought them inside — no charge! Then I headed off to the woods to begin my real job. Perhaps

Jule Caddell didn't understand how motivated I would be by my 1 cent per bottle bounty, and I'm sure he had no idea how many bottles had been thrown into the woods. He really had nothing to lose because the 1 cent per bottle he was going to give me would be returned to him by the soft drink delivery man later the same day. A couple of hours later I emerged from the woods with my clothes absolutely filthy and with a few scratches from black jack oaks and a little barbed wire, but I had retrieved 33 bottles. Some were clean as a whistle but most were full of dirt and leaves, so I cleaned each bottle at the pump behind the house before proudly taking them to the store where I would no doubt be received with great appreciation. Yeah, right!

After I dutifully placed the bottles into the proper wooden cartons, I proudly announced that I had found 33 bottles in the woods. Jule Caddell reluctantly handed me a quarter, a nickel and three pennies. I do believe that was the shiniest quarter I had ever seen, and I quickly dashed to Grandmother Caddell to have her put it away for me. I returned to the store to spend my remaining 8 cents when I heard good old Jule Caddell say to a customer, "He probably stole half of those bottles from me, and now I've got to buy them back." Boy, did he know how to break a little boy's heart! I put my 8 cents back in my pocket, and later in the day I went to Mr. Bud Hudson's store for my reward. At least he was always nice to me.

When Granddad McKinnon and I had our next visit, I told him about the way Jule Caddell always treated me. He seemed to listen even more closely than usual. He could easily see how my feelings were hurt. He told me that he guessed some things must be bothering old Jule Caddell. He said he suspected that the only reason Jule Caddell didn't like me was because he didn't take time to get to know me. He figured that if Jule knew me, even a little bit, he would like me a lot. He went on to say that, "I think I know you pretty good, and I sure do like you." There was that wink and smile again that I loved so much. Without saying anything, I slipped my hand into his and laid my head on his shoulder.

The Sitting & Talking Place

The sitting and talking place

Sometime between the time Granddad got home from the mill (around 2:12 PM) and supper time (around 6:00 PM), it was a pretty good bet that the two of us would head off to the store for a soft drink. The store was close enough that you could see it from the front porch, but it seemed like a long walk with bare feet on the hot crushed cinder street. Somewhere along the way, I would ask Granddad to hold my hand. He always agreed, but sometimes he would chuckle and ask if holding his hand made the road any cooler or any easier on my feet. Somehow it seemed to. After a while I didn't ask if he'd hold my hand. I'd just look up at him and hold my little hand up, and he would take it into his big strong hand.

The routine was always the same. He would get a Coca Cola and take a Goody powder, which he swore was the reason he never got sick. I would have a big old bottle of Pepsi Cola with a bag of salted peanuts poured inside. After speaking to whoever might be in the store, we quietly went to our favorite place — a shady, grassy spot out back facing the Safie ball park.

Most of the textile league games were played at night or on weekends, but sometimes we could hear the crack of the bat or the ball hitting the glove while the team practiced. The mill team was a source of great pride, and it was common for the company to bring in outstanding baseball players to work in the mill just to have them play for the company team. Everyone knew not to expect much work from those players, especially the day of a big game. Granddad claimed to not be a big baseball fan, but he knew all the players on the Safie team and could pick them out from our "sitting and talking place," even though it was a long ways away. He always encouraged me to keep playing baseball because the best players could always get a good job in the mill.

It was sitting on this particular piece of ground that I learned so much from Granddad. I will never know how many mistakes I avoided or how much I learned about family values, honesty and other life principles because of my many sessions with Granddad. He didn't talk much to other people, but he always opened up his heart to me freely and answered my unending string of questions as honestly as he knew how. He also took time to listen to me and never shied away from giving me a quiet but stern lecture whenever he thought I needed it. He taught me to honor my parents, to love my family, to be honest and to try to do my very best, whatever I was doing, but especially in school. Although he only attended school briefly, he knew the difference between an A and a C, and he quietly demanded A's from me. When I ran into a brick wall along life's way, his response was always the same. He asked if I had done my best. If I had, it was all right. If not, I knew what I had to do.

Sitting together, talking about the good things and the not so good things in our lives, we couldn't possibly know how important we were to each other — but I know now! Thank God, for Grandfathers!

 The Sitting & Talking Place

The driving lesson

My uncle, Archie McKinnon, who was a few years younger than mama, was bald but beautiful! He was always well dressed and looked like a million dollars. He had a great personality and women adored him. He also was the world's greatest fisherman. He married a lovely woman and had two daughters, but the marriage eventually failed. Although the broken marriage hurt him deeply, he hid it well. He moved back in with Granddad and Ma, who seemed delighted to have him around. He was always gracious to both of them and became their unofficial chauffeur.

Archie always had a really nice car which he kept cleaned and polished at all times. He said, "You never know when a beautiful girl will want to go for a ride." He also was kind enough to let all the younger guys in the family drive his car on special occasions over the years. He only had three rules about using his car. If you drove it, you washed it. If you drove it five miles or fifty, you returned it with a full tank of gas. If you scratched it, you died. Obviously, everyone was very careful with his car.

Granddad's house sat on a bit of a slope with the end nearest the garden sitting just off the ground while the other end was several feet high. The house was not underpinned and sat on brick columns, which made a great place under the house to hide from adults, as well as for catching doodle bugs. Uncle Archie always parked his car next to the high side of the house. He said he wanted it just outside his bedroom so it was the last thing he saw before going to bed at night and the first thing he saw when he got up in the morning.

One day Granddad told Uncle Archie it was time for 16 year old Uncle Don to learn to drive and that Uncle Archie was the one to teach him. Uncle Archie didn't seem to mind and, in fact, agreed to get right to work on it. For the next several days Uncle Archie talked (and talked, and talked) and Don listened. Don has always been a lot like Granddad and had very little to say. Finally, after Archie explained everything you could possibly want to know about automobiles and driving, it was time for Don to get behind the wheel. Ma and

Granddad stood proudly on the front porch, Loyce and Joyce were watching from the shade of the chinaberry tree and Bobby and I crawled into the backseat. Archie got in on the passenger side and Don slid nervously behind the wheel. Archie barked out directions and Don followed the orders perfectly. Archie said, "Put the key into the ignition, place one foot on the clutch and the other on the gas pedal. Now turn the key." Archie forgot to mention one small thing — make sure the car is out of gear. Unfortunately, it was also a very important thing! It was Don's intention to back up, but instead the car lurched forward. It seems that Archie had parked particularly close to the house the night before because we slammed into the side of the house, just missing the brick columns. We all were a little stunned, Don was embarrassed to death and Archie almost had a heart attack. As we piled out of the car, Granddad came walking up to Archie and said, "I believe he's got the going forward part down pretty good. If you work on the backing up a little bit, I think he'll have it."

It was months before Uncle Don tried driving again — in a big old field without a house in sight.

Big Red

W ith our three year difference, Uncle Bobby was more like an older brother than an uncle. Before Mama and Daddy got a house of their own in Roberdel, we lived together for nearly five years and always spent a lot of time together. It was alongside Bobby that I learned a lot about life. He used to tell every kid in his neighborhood that I was the meanest kid in Roberdel, and that when I came over to visit him, I would probably whip every one of them before I left Safie. Then I would arrive at Safie on Saturday and have to fight half the kids in the neighborhood just to prove my manhood.

Bobby and I sort of specialized in animal knowledge. For example, we discovered that two cats who had been friends since birth and who spent all of their time playing or sleeping together did not like one another very much when their tails were tied together. We also proved several times that no matter how hot the weather, sleeping hound dogs never appreciated having a bucket of cold water poured on them. We proved beyond a shadow of doubt that a cat will, indeed, eat a goldfish. Regrettably, we proved too many times, even after Granddad's warnings, that we were no match for Big Red, the meanest rooster who ever lived.

Bobby and I spent hours watching Big Red so we knew his every move. Our favorite activity was to crawl on top of the chicken house and wait on Big Red to come close enough so we could drop a bushel basket over him and leave him there until he was able to dig himself out, or Granddad rescued him. Other times we would drop a few pieces of chicken scratch feed outside the chicken lot and crack the door just enough for him to get out to eat the feed, and then we'd lock him outside. The fool rooster would almost kill himself trying to get back into the lot with his hens. Later when we finally got a water hose, he, of course, became our favorite target. You can bet he never got too dirty when we were around. Still, he pranced around like some sort of royalty looking over his domain.

Practically every time Bobby and I were together, we incurred Granddad's wrath about the way we treated Big Red. Finally, everything came to a climax. Bobby and I had decided to see if you could actually scare a rooster to death. Our plan was simple. Bobby would hide behind the hen house, then I would run right straight at Big Red screaming my head off. The rooster would figure that I had gone mad and would run around behind the chicken house. Then Bobby would jump out and holler as loud as he could, probably scaring Big Red to death. To set this little trap we tossed out a few pieces of chicken scratch feed, and when Big Red was eating and paying us no attention, I ran at him like a crazy man, yelling at the top of my lungs. Instead of being frightened, Big Red thought his manhood was being challenged in front of his hens. Rather than being afraid, he charged right at me with his wings spread at their maximum. I was terrified, so I turned and ran screaming for help. Bobby came running as fast as he could from the other direction, and we hit head on at the corner of the hen house. Fortunately, there wasn't any serious damage resulting from our collision. The cut in my head didn't require stitches, and Bobby's tooth was already loose.

We went inside and told Ma how Big Red had suddenly attacked us for no reason, while she cleaned our cuts and bruises. Bobby asked Granddad to see if he could find his tooth so that he might put it under his pillow in hopes the Tooth Fairy might leave him a dime for it. After a while, Granddad came back in the house chuckling. He was unable to find the tooth. Apparently Big Red thought it was scratch feed and had eaten it!

A McKinnon Christmas

Christmas was a wonderful time of the year for our family. The mill would close for at least a week and sometimes two. This gave all of us more family time together and eliminated dropping kids off here and there for a few days. The company sent bags of fruit and a toy for each child. Each worker received a Christmas bonus, although a small one. We went into the woods and cut a cedar tree and dragged it home for Mama's approval. Perfect Christmas trees from the North Carolina mountains hadn't found their way to Richmond County yet, and we simply cut the fullest tree we could find, turned the ugly side towards the wall and put decorations on the pretty side. While it was exciting to put the tree up and decorate it, we were more interested in the presents underneath.

Each little part of our family had its own Christmas celebration in our individual homes, and Santa Claus came to each house as well. But the happiest part of Christmas was going to Ma and Granddad's house on Christmas Eve. Everybody was there — Ma and Granddad, Uncle Archie and his wife Doris and their two daughters, Uncle Hayden, his wife Daisy and their son and daughter, Uncle Don (and later his wife, Janice, and their three girls), Loyce and Joyce (and later their husbands and children), Uncle Bobby, Mama, Daddy, my little brother Danny and me. There was more food than you could possibly imagine, and at least one group of carolers would come by to sing to us from the front yard. There were dozens of presents for everybody and we all started arriving by 6 PM. After eating our Christmas meal, the kids were all ready to open presents but not just yet. Somebody always had to take Ma to the Christmas Eve service at the Community Church at Hannah Pickett. No one was allowed to touch, shake, nor open a single present until Ma returned home from church. An hour can be a long time when you've been watching presents pile under Ma and Granddad's tree several weeks before Christmas.

Finally, Ma would get home and the fun began. We didn't draw names. Everybody bought a present for everybody and it was always just what they dreamed for, or so it seemed. I always felt a little sorry for Granddad because he never got anything to play with, except maybe an occasional flashlight or knife. He always got a carton or two of Lucky Strike cigarettes, a few dress shirts and several pairs of work pants. Once or twice I wrapped up a few fishing bobbers, a little line and a few hooks for him so he wouldn't be too disappointed.

The strangest thing happened every year. It would be getting late and everybody was getting tired, but we couldn't leave before Santa came to visit. He always showed up, but he never came inside. He just looked in the window and waved at us. Unfortunately, Uncle Archie never saw him one time over the many years. He would have to go to the store, or check on his car, or go to the bathroom, and wouldn't you know it, he missed Santa again. Since I was the oldest grandchild, I finally started to connect Uncle Archie's disappearance with the appearance of Santa Claus. I quietly confided in Granddad that I thought Uncle Archie might be Santa Claus. The next Christmas about the time Santa was supposed to show up, I went over and sat on Uncle Archie's lap to be sure he couldn't go outside. To my surprise, Santa showed up right on schedule, so that proved my suspicions to be wrong.

I ran to tell Granddad the good news that there really was a Santa Claus, but he had gone out back to check on his chickens.

Don't put eggs in your pocket

When I was spending the evenings with Ma and Granddad, I always wanted to help out around the garden or the kitchen, because if I did a really good job, I might get a Pepsi Cola out of the deal.

One afternoon it was obvious that Granddad didn't need my help because he was going to town with Uncle Archie to "pay a few bills." Granddad always paid his bills on time and in cash. He once told me that he always paid his bills when he had the money, but if the mill was on "short time" and he didn't have enough money, he'd "go down one side of the street paying and the other side of the street apologizing."

He left Ma and me to fix the supper. I soon asked Ma what I could do to help, and she told me to go to the chicken house out back and get her four eggs. Her last words were, "Do not put the eggs in your pockets." What a foolish thing to say to someone as smart as me.

The job seemed easy enough, but the hens didn't do their part. I quickly found three eggs and one of them was so fresh it was still warm, but Ma had said she needed four eggs. I noticed that one hen was sitting on a nest so I figured if I waited a minute or two she would produce the fourth egg. I scurried around outside and found the feed bucket that we used to carry the scratch feed, and I flipped it over and made myself a stool. I then sat down in the chicken house and waited. A few minutes is a long time when you're seven years old, especially when your Grandma is waiting for four eggs, not to mention the fact that a chicken house is a pretty dirty and smelly place. I suppose I ran my hand under the old hen 10 or 12 times over the next few minutes. I know it was enough to make the chicken so upset that she wasn't about to lay an egg. Realizing that the hen needed my help, I picked her up and shook her. Having no luck I then squeezed her a little to help her push her egg out. No luck! I finally decided that the hen obviously didn't understand how much we needed this egg so I tried to talk her into laying the egg. I got up real close to the chicken and told her that Ma was waiting in the kitchen for four eggs and that she needed them right now. The hen sort of cocked her head a little and seemed to understand the problem. I then realized that she was trying to decide exactly where to peck me because she nailed me right on the tip of my nose. It hurt so badly it brought tears to my eyes, but what really hurt was the sinking feeling I had as I jumped backwards and fell on the ground. As I got up I felt the sticky eggs running down my pants leg. Everybody knows that when a boy is busy using both hands to help a chicken lay an egg that the only place to put the other eggs is in his pockets.

As I waddled inside to tell my tale of woe, Granddad came walking in, took one look at me, and said, "Looks like we might need to borrow a few eggs from our neighbors." Later, after a great supper, wearing a pair of Uncle Bobby's pants and with a bandage on my nose, I was able to laugh with Ma and Granddad about my adventure. As he headed to bed, Granddad asked me what I had learned that day. My response was quick, "It doesn't do any good to try to talk to a chicken, chickens don't need any help laying eggs and don't ever put eggs in your pocket. Good night, Granddad."

The biggest nose in America

Most of the shade at Granddad's house was provided by a couple of chinaberry trees with one really big one almost completely providing cover for the back yard. This single tree was a source of some of our finest (and not so finest) adventures. Bobby and I would climb to the very top of the tree and then drop 100 or so chinaberries on whoever walked beneath us. Our favorite targets were my twin aunts — Loyce and Joyce — and their friends. Everybody knew that girls couldn't climb trees so all they could do was stand on the ground and yell at us. I must admit they were pretty good at screaming but no good at all at throwing, so we let them have it every chance we got. A chinaberry also fits very nicely into a slingshot, so Bobby and I could make the cats move along pretty well, too. The shade provided a great place to shoot marbles, play catch or throw the knife. I think it's safe to say that when we weren't working in the garden or looking after the chickens, most of our time was spent in this shady little playground.

One day when we must have really gotten bored, Bobby put a chinaberry up each of his nostrils. It was pretty funny. In fact we discovered that the further up into your nostril you pushed the chinaberry, the funnier it looked. When Bobby put two chinaberries in each nostril, I thought I'd pass out from laughter. You could just imagine how hilarious it was when I managed to get eight chinaberries in each nostril. Bobby went inside and got a mirror so we both could enjoy this unusual sight — this skinny, black haired little kid with a big red nose full of chinaberries. In fact, we rode up and down Fifth Street on our bikes to proudly show off "the biggest nose in America." I don't think Bobby was ever prouder of me.

When it came time for dinner, I started taking the tightly fitted chinaberries out of my now very sore and swollen nose. The first 10 or 12 came out fine but each nostril was quite irritated and throbbing with pain. Panic is never a good thing but especially when deep breathing simply isn't possible. Finally, I went into the bedroom and lay flat on my back on Granddad's bed while Bobby tried to get the chinaberries dislodged by using a pair of pliers, a flat headed screwdriver and a fork. Fortunately, before Bobby had time to kill me, Granddad walked into the bedroom and calmly told Bobby to go tell Ma to bring some warm water and a clean cloth. It took him only a few minutes to get all but one of the chinaberries free. In the meantime two or three neighborhood boys had come by to fight the "meanest kid from Roberdel" and Bobby told them that they'd have to come back later because right now his Daddy was operating on the Roberdel kid. By the time the word got around the neighborhood, at least 10 or 12 aspiring young surgeons were witnessing the operation. Just before giving up and calling the doctor, Granddad was able to remove the last chinaberry with the help of a reedhook, a long, skinny tool used to pull yarn through a piece of textile machinery.

All in all it turned out to be a pretty interesting day. I made Uncle Bobby very proud of me, I survived my first surgery and the kids in the neighborhood thought I was a pretty cool dude. However, my nose was too sore to fight for a few days and everything I ate for a week tasted like chinaberries.

 The Sitting & Talking Place

Catching chickens, one by one

Some of the biggest disasters in our lives seem to result from some of our most honorable intentions. Ma had told me that Granddad wasn't feeling so great when he left for work one morning, so I decided I would take care of some of the chores that usually awaited him when he got home from work. I went out and watered the chickens and brought in all the freshly laid eggs. This all seemed to go very well, and I couldn't wait for Granddad to get home and see what I had done for him.

When I saw him coming through the backyard, I was prepared to be thanked by my tired, but grateful, Granddad. The first words out of his mouth were, "How did the chickens get out of the lot?" In my haste to have these important jobs completed before Granddad got home, I had forgotten to latch the door to the chicken lot. Since I was responsible for the chickens getting out, I quickly replied, "Don't worry! I'll catch them for you." Since Granddad wasn't feeling too well anyway, he nodded his approval and went to get a Goody powder. About an hour later he came outside to find me red faced from chasing chickens and with only two of the twenty chickens back in the lot. There were feathers everywhere. Four chickens were in the top of the chinaberry tree, two on the hood of Uncle Archie's car, three on top of the house, two on the front porch and at least six under the house. Granddad surveyed the situation and observed, "Geeboy, you're trying to catch all the chickens at once, but you're going to have to catch them one at a time. That's how they got out." He was right, of course. With a handful of chicken scratch feed, I caught all the chickens but the three on top of the house within the next 30 minutes. Exhausted I went inside and confided to Granddad that I didn't know how to get the three hens off the roof top.

Obviously feeling better, he laughed when he told me to come with him, and he'd show me how to catch the other chickens. He grabbed up a handful of feed, walked into the chicken lot and started clucking like a hen. As soon as he started, every hen in sight, including the ones on the top of the house, perked up and started listening to him. Then he told me to open the chicken lot gate, and he clucked some more and started tossing the feed into the flock of hens around him. The three chickens on the top of the house quickly jumped down and ran inside the lot to join the others in their scramble for food.

I knew my Granddad was pretty special and that he loved his chickens, but it was the first time I realized that he could actually speak chicken talk.

Putting in a garden

In the early spring Granddad would get out his plow, the one with the big wheel, and oil it up and prepare for planting his garden. He would get someone at the mill who had a horse or a mule to come by and "break up" his garden spot. Then he would go to work pulling weeds and grass until he was ready to put his push plow to work. He always let me help clean up the garden spot before it was plowed and pull weeds and grass afterwards. The spring wasn't very hot and it was amazing how dirty you could get working in the garden. The best part was that no one seemed to care.

It seemed to me that his garden was about 1 mile wide and 2 or 3 miles deep. It actually was about 40 feet wide and 120 feet deep. When the garden spot was perfectly cleaned off, and properly broken up, Granddad would push his hand plow through the garden spot several times. After pulling every blade of grass and every weed, it was off to the feed store or hardware to get some seeds and plants. Granddad never left anything about his garden to chance. He had exactly the right number of tomato plants, as well as the perfect number of seeds for butter beans, peas, green beans, corn, cucumbers, peppers and okra. When planting day was scheduled for Saturday, I was allowed to spend the night before at Granddad and Ma's house. We were awakened bright and early by Big Red, the meanest rooster who ever lived, who crowed loudly at the first sign of daylight. After Granddad had breakfast and I slept 30 more minutes, we went out to the garden spot. My job was to carry a bucket of water and a dipper. Granddad would plant the tomato plants and put seeds in the ground, and I would cover the seeds and put a dipper of water on each plant and each bunch of seeds. Only after I was much older was I allowed to do any actual planting. I suspect that Granddad could have done his planting a lot quicker if I had not been there to help, but a boy has to learn sooner or later how to "put in" a garden. It took all morning and a good part of the afternoon to completely plant the garden, but we knew that a few weeks down the road we would have plenty of fresh vegetables to show for our work. We would only take one short break during the morning, and there was no time for a trip to the store for a soft drink. We would just have a little sit down under the shade of the chinaberry tree in the back yard and enjoy a glass of water and maybe a country ham biscuit. However, every time I had to refill the water bucket, I would manage to spill a dipper full somewhere near my mouth and down my bare chest.

We must have been something to see when planting the garden. Granddad working so hard, quietly and precisely planting the garden for his family, and me yapping 100 words a minute and dragging my water bucket up one row and down the other. I always found Granddad to be a good partner for conversation, I talked and he listened — or at least appeared to listen. He would raise his eyebrows or nod his head enough for me to think he was enjoying his end of the conversation as much as I was enjoying mine.

When it seemed that we had planted about 2 million tomato plants, I asked him why we were planting so many. He stopped a minute, took his hat off and wiped his sweating head with his handkerchief. He pointed to the first row of plants and said, "Those tomatoes are for your Grandmother and me and our younguns." The next row he reminded me were, "For your Mama and Daddy and your family as well as your uncles and their families." The last row, he explained, was, "For our neighbors."

I can't begin to explain how much pride I took in the garden Granddad and I planted, tended and harvested together, pulling grass and weeds all spring and summer, especially after it got so hot. It was no easy job, but the reward of watching our families and neighbors enjoying the vegetables made it all worthwhile.

Sure enough, when the tomatoes started getting ripe, Granddad and I would take a bunch of his small brown lunch bags out to the garden. He would carefully pick the ripe tomatoes, gently wiping the sand from them and put two or three in each bag. Then I would take my bike and go up and down Fifth Street putting a bag of tomatoes on the front porch of every house. We didn't have to tell them who left them there. They knew they were from their neighbor, Will McKinnon and his grandson. I can still feel the cool, freshly plowed dirt between my bare toes.

A day at Ledbetter

Granddad took advantage of every opportunity to work overtime. When he worked on Saturday or extra hours during the week, he was paid 1 1/2 times his usual hourly wage. This was the way he saved up a little money for Christmas and other special occasions. However, a couple of Saturdays were set aside each year for an all day trip to Ledbetter, another mill village north of Rockingham, to visit with Ma's relatives, the Curries and the Lovins.

One Friday I spent the night with them, so I could accompany them on one of those trips. We got up early, had a good breakfast and piled in Uncle Archie's car. We went to Aunt Nancy and Uncle Tave Lovin's house which sat beside Ledbetter Lake near the bridge above the dam. Uncle Tave kept the yard full of homemade wooden boats, which he rented to fishermen. Granddad, Uncle Archie and I joined Uncle Tave under a shade tree down by the lake where he collected fees from the aspiring anglers. Ma went inside and joined her sister Nancy and the other ladies who had gathered to visit.

Most of our visits to Ledbetter were on Sunday so we were usually too dressed up to fish, but today was Saturday, and we came prepared to fish all day. In fact, the men of the village had decided to have a big fish stew later in the afternoon if we caught enough fish.

Pretty soon after we arrived, Uncle Kennie Currie pulled up in his boat and picked up Granddad. Archie, Bobby and I followed in one of Uncle Tave's boats. Tave said, "You boys can have the boat free of charge, if you bring back a mess of fish, but if you come back empty handed, you'll have to pay double." I knew we would catch plenty of fish because Archie was the greatest fisherman who ever lived and Uncle Kennie knew exactly where every fish in Ledbetter Lake lived as well as what they liked to eat. A third boat soon joined us with John, Malcolm, and Kennie Lovin — all heavily armed with fishing gear. We caught so many fish I lost count, but enough that we didn't have to pay rent on the boat and plenty to feed all of our relatives, which included everybody in the Ledbetter village. The fish were cooked in two big black pots along with fresh tomatoes, onions, potatoes and okra to form a splendid fish stew. It was served with sweetened iced tea and cornbread. We also enjoyed a churn of homemade ice cream for dessert.

Of course, everybody graciously thanked all the fishermen and at the end of the evening the ladies presented a newly stitched quilt to Ma. Uncle Archie dropped me off at home as they passed through Roberdel. I hated to see this day end because it was perfect in every way. As I laid in bed that night, I thought about how lucky I was to spend such a special day with the people who loved me the most — my family. Sleep came easily that night.

A boy and his dog

We moved into a larger house right in the center of Roberdel when I was 10 years old. It was on the Roberdel Pond and was a great place to grow up. Given that it was on the corner of Roberdel Road and Hudson Street, it was no place to raise a pet, but Heaven knows my little brother, Danny, and I tried. Roberdel Road was very busy and used frequently by youngsters who had just received their driving licenses. When their parents were present, they observed even the most minor traffic law, but when they were alone — watch out! It seemed that every few months one of them drove their car into the pine tree on the corner of our lot. Of course, their insurance companies always paid Mama a little something for damages. In fact, it happened so often that Mama called the tree her "money tree." Sometimes when she needed a new dress or a rocking chair, she would patiently wait for someone else to hit "the money tree" — and sure enough, before long, it would happen.

The other side of the property was a death trap for pets. Speeding teenage drivers or retired textile workers who had given their eyesight to the company through years of tying tiny knots or carefully inspecting cloth couldn't see nor react quickly enough to avoid a collision with a lazy hound dog who thought he owned Hudson Street.

Somehow we learned to deal with losing our pet dogs over the years, but my favorite nearly died for a different reason. A lonely old man filled with venom announced at Hudson's Grocery Store one Saturday morning that a dog in the neighborhood had killed one of his chickens and that he was "pretty sure" it belonged to Marshall Caddell's boy — "not his real son, but that other one he's raising." Mr. Bud Hudson disagreed and told him, "It must be somebody else's dog, because the little McGee boy takes good care of his dog. It takes a hungry dog to kill chickens, and that boy feeds his dog two or three times a day."

However, when the news reached our home, Daddy sat me down and told me about the remark by the "old fellow from Hogback Street." He said he knew Mac was my favorite pet, but if he was killing chickens, we would have to get rid of him. Predictably, I stood by my dog and promised to watch him more closely.

On Monday, as always, Mama and Daddy dropped me off at Ma and Granddad's home when they went to work. As soon as I saw Granddad, I started talking 200 miles an hour about my dog being blamed for something he didn't do. Granddad told me that no matter how much you loved a hound dog, he was still just a hound dog. He said that even the best pets could make a mistake, especially if he got hungry. I told him there was no way my dog had been hungry because I fed him three or four times a day, and he had gotten "fat as a hog." After Granddad had a good chuckle, he said, "We need to sit on this situation a while, and we'll think of something to do." After supper he asked me who had said it was my dog and what day of the week he had said it. I told him the man's name and told him that it was Saturday morning that he accused my dog and me. Obviously, I had taken his words personally. So we put together a little plan and promised that neither of us would tell a soul.

The next Saturday morning, the men gathered at Bud Hudson's store, as usual. This Saturday they had a visitor from East Rockingham — Willie C. McKinnon. Mr. Hudson knew Granddad, but to the others he was just somebody who had probably come to Roberdel for a day of fishing. Pretty soon the "old fellow from Hogback Street" arrived, and, sure enough, he announced that the dog had attacked his hen house again. Although he sure hated to, he said he was "going to Marshall Caddell's house and kill that scoundrel of a dog." The visiting gentleman asked if the fellow was absolutely sure that the little boy's dog had killed his chickens because it would be mighty upsetting to the little boy to lose his dog. The old fellow said he was "damn sure it was his dog, because this time I saw him leaving my yard." Agreeing that killing chickens should be a capital offense, if you have the right dog, Granddad agreed to go with him down the street to the Caddell home.

A sharp knock brought Mary and Marshall Caddell to the door. I quickly joined them. Granddad, acting like he had never seen any of us, announced that the other gentleman had had a problem with a dog killing his chickens and that he had seen their dog leaving his yard "about midnight last night."

It didn't seem exactly right for a smile to blanket the face of a little boy about to lose his favorite dog. Before anybody else spoke, Granddad asked the gentleman again if he was absolutely sure about the identity of the dog and if it was actually last night that the attack occurred. The "old fellow from Hogback" was quick to respond "Yes" to both questions. At this point Daddy asked me if I knew where my dog was and I couldn't wait to answer, "Yes sir! He's in my bed. He slept with me last night."

It was at this point that the accuser made his worst mistake. He blurted out, "It's obvious that the boy's lying. He just let the dog in the house this morning to protect it." Granddad calmly looked the fellow in the eye with a gaze of pity. He said, "Mister, I just met you an hour ago, but I've known this little boy since the day he was born. He's never told me one lie about anything, and you've already told me a half a dozen. Now I could understand a little boy lying to protect his dog, but I can't imagine a grown man lying just to hurt a little boy. You owe this little boy and his dog an apology for accusing them. Now, the only question is, are you going to apologize now or after I kick your sorry, lying tail up and down Hudson Street?"

Apology accepted.

The Sitting & Talking Place

The Sitting & Talking Place

Our first game of pool

From my grandparents' front porch you could see both of the little neighborhood stores. One was a very nice grocery store which was always filled with folks picking up a few items for their families or sitting around enjoying a soft drink and bantering with friends and neighbors. Vulgar language was never heard there. The building was kept very clean as were the surrounding grounds, including the spot Granddad and I used for our little talks about life.

The other store was always full of men who sat around drinking beer and shooting pool. Nothing but vulgar language seemed to be used by these hardened fellows, and the only time their loud talk and dirty jokes stopped was when a woman or child ran in to pick up a loaf of bread or bottle of milk. No sooner than they were out the door, the colorful language picked back up. As you might imagine, the pool hall was strictly off limits for Uncle Bobby and me.

Often Ma would ask Bobby and me to run to the store to pick up an item or two for her. We were glad to do it because it gave us a reason to grab our bikes and head out on an adventure. Usually Ma would give us a little more money than we needed and tell us to "keep the change" which would be our bounty for helping her out a little and for being perfect little angels. Usually the change was only 10 or 20 cents, but that was enough for a couple of soft drinks or ice creams.

It's true that sometimes little boys get a piece of information that they probably would be better off without. In our case, we had discovered that you could shoot a game of pool for 10 cents. Now this was clearly information we should not have had because we immediately began developing a plan to get our hands on a dime and go shoot a game of pool at the "other" neighborhood store — the pool hall!

Since the pool hall was visible from Ma's front porch, as well as in plain view for her tattletale neighbors, we pulled our bikes behind the pool hall next to the railroad tracks. Then we entered from the rear and quietly started watching a couple of men shoot a few games of pool. After figuring out basically how the game worked, we fished around in our pockets, plunked our dime on the counter and announced that we had come to shoot a game of pool. The owner of the pool hall took our 10 cents and we started shooting. We discovered pretty quickly that watching a game of pool is much easier than shooting one, but after a while we finished our game. We carefully put our pool sticks away, slipped out the back door, grabbed our bikes and headed home. We had successfully shot a game of pool, and absolutely no one knew it but us. Life was good!

Later that evening after helping Granddad with his chores, we all cleaned up for supper. It had been quite a day and Bobby, and I started snickering every time we looked at one another because we knew we had pulled off the perfect crime. We were both really hungry because pool shooting and doing chores makes boys ready to eat. Ma had prepared fried chicken, peas and butter beans, fresh tomatoes, corn on the cob, homemade biscuits and iced tea. Just as we sat down to eat, there was a loud knock on the front door, and Granddad went to see who our visitor might be. From the opened door we heard a man's voice say, "Mr. McKinnon, I brought your grandson's baseball cap. He left it at my store today when he and Bobby came by to shoot pool."

Suddenly, I wasn't hungry any more.

The Sitting & Talking Place

My first job

On a lazy summer afternoon Granddad and I picked a few vegetables and delivered them to Ma's kitchen where in just a couple of hours they would be transformed into something wonderful and delicious. He then looked at me and said those magic words, "Geeboy, do you want to go to the store?" "Do, I?" With the unspoken promise of a 12 ounce Pepsi and a pack of salted peanuts, I was ready to go in a flash.

We sat behind the store in our "sitting and talking place" talking a little bit about school, playing ball and such stuff. "Granddad, there's something I need real bad," I said.

"What's that?" he asked. "It looks to me like you've got just about everything a boy could want."

"Yes, sir. But I need a Boy Scout uniform and money to go to church camp in the mountains. I think I need a job. What do you think I could do?"

"Well, you're pretty good at gardening and Ma says you're a pretty good dishwasher, but those jobs don't pay very much. What else can you do?"

I replied quickly, "I can read pretty good, and Mrs. McDonald says I'm the best speller in my class."

"Well" he replied, "I suspect you know everybody in Roberdel by now and you've got a pretty good bicycle. How about getting you a paper route?"

Now everybody knew my Granddad was a pretty smart fellow, so the next day Daddy and I started looking for a paper route in Roberdel. Unfortunately, only two afternoon papers were delivered in Roberdel at that time — The Charlotte News and The Richmond County Journal — and both had carriers already. However, they needed someone to sell the Grit, a weekly paper. So I started selling the Grit and I sold a lot of them, but the distributor soon went out of business, and my first job didn't last very long. Luck was with me though, and before

The Sitting & Talking Place

long I was able to get the job of delivering The Charlotte News six afternoons a week.

I quickly discovered that the more customers you had, the more money you made. I also found out that even when it rained, your customers expected to get their papers. That was fine by me. A little rain had never hurt anybody. Pretty soon my customers grew from 18 to 30 and finally to 42. Before you knew it, I had my Boy Scout uniform, and I was off to Ridgecrest Baptist Assembly without using Mama and Daddy's hard earned money.

As the paper company kept introducing new incentives for carriers who found new customers, my route became longer and longer. In fact, from one end to the other it now covered nearly three miles. I was rewarded nicely for my growing number of customers as I had now more than doubled my income. In addition to winning a baseball bat, I won saddle bags for my bike and the first camera our family ever owned. I needed one more new customer to win the grand prize in one of the contests, and Daddy thought Jule Caddell might take the paper's deal of eight weeks at half price. Of course, Jule decided he didn't need "no fool newspaper." How silly of me. He already knew everything.

He probably wouldn't have paid me anyway.

212 assorted pieces of the very best fishing equipment

All the McKinnon men loved to fish. Since we lived on the Roberdel pond, most Saturdays found at least a few of them fishing in our backyard. The secret to our success was simple — we always put table scraps into a burlap bag, closed the bag tightly and tied a rope to the bag of scraps. Then we would toss the bag out into the water and tie the rope to a tree stump. The fish (and turtles and snakes) would suck the food through the tiny holes in the burlap sack. This was called "baiting" a fishing hole. When we wanted to fish, we'd pull the bag of food out of the water and toss our lines in. I suppose a fish which had been trying to get food from a burlap sack found a juicy looking worm pretty attractive. We could always expect to catch all the fish we wanted to clean and eat. You can't possibly imagine all the strange things we caught. They included catfish, bream, crappie, suckers, perch, bass, jacks, eels and snapping turtles. We all have our favorite fishing stories, and one of Granddad's was when my little brother, Danny, caught his first little turtle and yelled, "Somebody come help me, I think I've caught an alligator!"

Most of the McKinnon clan slowly moved from fishing with bamboo poles and cork bobbers to fishing rods and reels from the new store. Although they seemed to catch more fish than us, Granddad and I stuck to the bamboo poles, which grew plentifully on the bank between our house and the pond. We always kept a half dozen or so ready for use and a handful more cut and drying out so that they would be ready to replace the ones which got broken by the gyrations of a big eel or jack that didn't particularly enjoy being on the end of our line, or by someone stepping on the pole and breaking off the tip.

Finally, one year on Granddad's birthday, Uncle Archie, the greatest fisherman of all time, bought him a fishing rod and reel and a tackle box absolutely full of fancy lures, spinners and hooks. In fact, the advertisement said, "New rod and reel with 212 assorted pieces of the very best fishing equipment." Since his birthday was in early November, we had to wait until the next spring to try out the new rod and reel. We talked all winter about the fish not standing a chance against Granddad and his new equipment. Heck, Granddad and I figured that we would probably catch so many fish that we'd have to give some of them to our friends and neighbors, or better yet, sell them to the folks downtown.

The Sitting & Talking Place

Slowly, the winter passed and spring finally arrived. On the Saturday of the full moon in April, Granddad and Archie showed up early in the morning for the great unveiling of Granddad's rod and reel and "212 assorted pieces of the very best fishing equipment." I should note here that neither my Granddad nor I were known for our patience. While Uncle Archie was explaining how to cast the rod and reel to the exact spot where the fish would be eagerly awaiting the lure, Granddad was looking for his fish stringer and was wondering if it had room for all the fish he would catch. Realizing he didn't have a very interested student, Uncle Archie soon gave up and handed the shiny new fishing rod and reel to Granddad and moved away to begin fishing himself. Granddad took about 10 seconds to look over the new equipment and let fly with his first cast. Unfortunately, he forgot to let go of the reel mechanism, and we had to deal with our first line backlash — and a fine one it was! Since my fingers were smaller and my eyesight a lot better than Granddad's, I went to work and soon had it untangled. Handing the rod and reel back to Granddad, I moved away to make sure he had room to operate. This attempt was much better, but the line went dead left instead of straight out into the pond. Rex, the latest in our long line of hound dogs, always went fishing with us, and he was curled up in the shade sound asleep. The plug with about 12 hooks hit him right at the base of his tail, and he let out a howl. Before he had run too far with the plug cleanly hooked into his backside, I wrestled him to the ground and performed minor surgery to remove the plug. Fortunately, only a couple of the barbs on the plug had to be removed. Only the look of puzzlement on Granddad's face kept me from falling on the ground in laughter.

Cast number three was every bit as entertaining. Just when it looked like the plug might actually hit the water, it went over a limb, which hung over the lake. I'm not exaggerating when I say that line must have wrapped around the end of that limb 20 times. Granddad looked at me, and I knew what I had to do. I climbed the tree and crawled out on the limb as far as possible and broke off the portion of the limb which held the line. Then we cut the line off and tied the plug back on to the new end of the line. Once again, we were in the fishing business.

By now Uncle Archie had moved to a fishing spot where Granddad couldn't see or hear him laughing and had landed four or five nice fish. Undaunted, Granddad took a deep breath and gave the rod and reel yet another mighty heave. In our excitement we had forgotten that sometimes the ground real close to the water got soft and mushy when you stood in the same place for too long. Just as Granddad cast, his foot slipped and down he went with one foot in the pond and one on the bank. There wasn't anything particularly unusual about this except it happened while casting. Later, we would decide it would have been a great cast if Granddad hadn't slipped and let go of the rod and reel. The rod and reel soared end over end a couple of times before splashing into the water and settling at its new home at the bottom of Roberdel pond. The two of us stood silently for a while as we watched the splash and the ripples on the smooth surface of the pond. Without saying anything, I picked up the hoe and started digging for earthworms while Granddad went to get us two bamboo poles. We caught two suckers, a jack, four catfish and an eel. Who needs a rod and reel and "212 assorted pieces of the very best fishing equipment?"

Rex, our hound dog, came back from the safety of the bamboo thicket, curled up between us and went back to sleep.

The Sitting & Talking Place

Knives are for big boys

One day, when I was about 11 or 12 years old, I was talking to Granddad about life's ups and downs. He made a casual comment about me growing up mighty quickly. I took advantage of this comment to ask, "How old does a boy have to be before he can have his own knife?" All the men in our family carried a pocket knife, and I thought it was about time I had one. My parents disagreed. Granddad thought a little bit and replied, "I don't guess there's any certain age. It depends on the boy. I've known some boys who were probably ready for a knife when they were about your age, but I've known grown men who were 50 years old that probably shouldn't carry a knife." He added, "I'll make a deal with you. I've got an extra knife or two around here. I'll let you use one when you're here visiting. If you'll be careful with it, keep it clean and always put it away before you go home, you can use it. If you can't do those things, you probably aren't quite ready to have a knife of your own yet." I accepted his offer, and he went to his personal trunk and let me choose one of his spare knives.

I picked a knife with two small blades and a shiny black case. For several weeks I was right on the spot anytime anyone needed to cut something. I tried to whittle a little, but mostly I just liked to reach in my pocket, feel the knife, and know it was there. I was growing up, and I could prove it because only a big kid was allowed to carry a knife. I kept it shiny clean and put it away safely each night.

A popular game among boys who owned knives was called, "throw the knife." It involved drawing a circle in the dirt and dividing the circle into equal halves. Then you gave each of two knife-owning boys half of the circle as his territory, and each had to stand in his half. Then they took turns throwing the opened knives at the other person's territory. If your knife stuck in the ground in your opponent's territory, you drew a line slicing off that much of his territory and adding it to yours. If your knife didn't stick in the ground, you lost your turn. There was a real art to throwing your knife in a fashion that allowed it to stick in the ground most of the time. When one person eventually owned so much territory that his opponent had nowhere to stand and throw, the game was over.

Since I had never owned a knife, I had never played the game, but now I could participate along with the older boys. They carefully went over the rules with me but forgot to mention it was a good idea to wear shoes when you played "throw the knife." Everything went fine for a while, but then I lost so much of my territory that I had to stand very awkwardly in order to get my foot into my territory for my throw. Being rather competitive, I pushed myself up on my toes and let fly with the knife. Technically, I guess I won the game because when the knife stuck directly upright in the meat of my foot, just below my second toe, blood flew everywhere and my opponent fainted. I suppose it was the only technical knock-out ever recorded in "throw the knife." I quickly pulled the knife blade from my foot. Uncle Bobby went to get Ma to help revive the other kid. I hobbled inside, cleaned up my foot and Granddad put a bandage on it.

The knife didn't cause a lot of pain. What really hurt was when Granddad said, "It looks like we might need to wait a while longer before you're ready to own a knife." I couldn't disagree. I carefully cleaned the knife, and Granddad put it back in its trunk. The next time I saw the knife was when I unwrapped it on my 16th birthday — a present from Granddad.

The Sitting & Talking Place

A long ride for a mean dog

Nobody likes mean dogs except the owners of the mean dogs. It seems that they are quick to defend their mutt even when it is obvious to everyone else that their dog creates problems for folks in their neighborhood. I am fortunate I spent most of my early years living and growing up in mill villages, but I promise you I've never seen a mill neighborhood that didn't have a few mean dogs, as well as a few irresponsible dog owners.

For the most part, the only time his neighbors ever saw any evidence of Will McKinnon was through the vegetables he had graciously left on their front porches. If he came calling, it was surely a sign of deep concern.

Fifth Street was a very shady street and a great place to ride bicycles. Uncle Bobby and I must have ridden thousands of miles up and down Fifth Street, and we knew practically everyone in the block. We considered it a very safe place to ride and play and certainly didn't think any harm could come to us during these activities. However, one day we were both startled when a large black dog ran from under a house and knocked me off of my bicycle. Before I could get away from him he had bitten me on the hip, and even though he did not cause an open wound, he created a noticeable bruise which lasted for quite some time.

A few weeks later, Uncle Archie's little girl, Carol, was spending the day with our Grandparents. Ma asked her to run over to a neighbor's house to borrow a carrot so she could finish the supper she was preparing. Carol asked which neighbor, and Ma said it really didn't matter. She told Carol just to pick a house because most anybody would have a carrot. Unfortunately, Carol picked the wrong house. She happily ran down the street and skipped up the front steps, without noticing the same big black dog laying on the porch. Just as she reached to knock on the door, the dog, which was at least as big as Carol, attacked her and bit her leg. She screamed and ran home, more frightened than hurt, but hurt nonetheless. Her screams scared the dog away and certainly saved Carol from further harm – maybe even saved her life. Still, the neighbor expressed no more concern about Carol than he did after the dog had bitten me.

A few minutes later Granddad walked up those same steps and knocked on the neighbor's door. When the man of the house appeared, he was surprised to see Will McKinnon. It was pretty obvious that Granddad hadn't dropped by to deliver any vegetables. He calmly said, "This is the second time your dog has hurt one of my grandchildren in the past few weeks. It's time for you to put your dog in a pen or tie him up to keep him from hurting other children." The neighbor bitterly replied, "That dog don't bother nobody that don't bother him." Granddad didn't spend any more time discussing the matter with his unresponsive neighbor.

Several evenings later we were all surprised when Uncle Archie and Granddad suddenly decided to take a late night ride "up towards the Pee Dee River hills." The neighbor's big black dog was never seen in the Safie Village again.

The Sitting & Talking Place

Ocean Drive vacation

My Grandfather wasn't one to venture far from East Rockingham except for an occasional visit to Roberdel or Ledbetter. Even on those infrequent visits, he didn't linger too long before returning home. On the other hand, if you casually mentioned going anywhere to Ma, it only took her a minute to get her hat and pocketbook, and she was ready to travel.

The mill always closed for a week for July 4th and each employee received a bonus which covered lost wages. A lot of the mill families traveled to the Carolina beaches or the Great Smoky Mountains for a few days, but Granddad and Ma always stayed home. This was due in part to the fact that they never owned a car, but mostly because Granddad didn't care to go anywhere. Although he was a little better than Granddad, my stepfather, Marshall Caddell, wasn't exactly a globetrotter himself.

When you're a child you can learn a lot from adults when they don't know you're listening. Playing around the kitchen I could see and hear a conspiracy brewing. Ma and Mama wanted to go to Ocean Drive Beach for July 4th. Granddad and Daddy fussed and complained about their gardens and a dozen other things which they had to do the week of July the 4th. They never had a chance. My little brother, Danny, my Uncle Bobby and I began packing a few toys and bathing suits because it was obvious to us early on that we were going to the beach.

Finally the men gave in, and we got ready to hit the road — all seven of us in one car! For some reason we left at 4 AM, and at 6:30 AM or thereabouts, I was awakened so that I could see the ocean just as the sun came up. It was absolutely beautiful, but quite frankly, I think I would have liked it better if it had it been a little later in the day. Back in those days you could actually drive your car on the Grand Strand, so we drove down the beach and watched the waves splashing ashore. After a little while, Daddy said, "Everybody take a good look. It's time to head back home." It was 7 AM and he figured we could be back by 10 AM. Granddad nodded his agreement, but the rest of us hit the ceiling. We thought we had come to stay a week!

Mama suggested that the three kids change into bathing suits and play in the waves, which were breaking near shore, while the adults had a little discussion. Amazingly, when our swim was over,

Mama announced that we were going to stay three nights in an apartment that was owned by some folks from Rockingham. The three kids almost went berserk we were so thrilled about the outcome of those negotiations.

We had the time of our lives — sand, sun and great food, not to mention that Danny, Bobby and I got to sleep together on a pallet on the floor. Then the commode in our apartment exploded! Water and other stuff was running everywhere. Every time we thought it was over, here it came again. Of course, between trips carrying stuff to the bathroom down the hall, the three kids thought it was the funniest thing that had ever happened. When we finally got everything cleaned up and the plumber came and fixed the commode, we went out for a great seafood supper and laughed until we almost passed out. Granddad said he hadn't seen that much manure since the last time he cleaned his hen house.

It was a great vacation, and the only one I remember Granddad and Ma ever taking.

The day Big Red died

W hen Granddad wasn't within hearing range, we had a lot of discussions about how much he loved old "Big Red," the meanest rooster that ever lived. We knew Granddad loved us, but we suspected that if he ever had to choose between us and Big Red, that he'd probably choose the rooster. He told us at least 100 times that a good rooster was not easy to find, and when you were lucky enough to have one, that you sure better take care of it. He said that a good rooster protected hens from snakes, dogs and most anything else — which probably meant little boys. He also said that if a rooster did his job, the hens would always lay plenty of eggs and give you an occasional yard full of baby chicks. Now, that was a big surprise, because I thought baby chicks came from the Easter bunny and that they came in a lot of different colors.

It seemed that when Big Red suddenly attacked Bobby and me for reasons we couldn't, or wouldn't explain, Granddad assumed that we had done something mean to the rooster. Imagine that! We could usually count on Ma's support when we had an occasional confrontation with Big Red, but Granddad was another story altogether.

Of course, Bobby and I were constantly trying to figure out how to kill Big Red without leaving any evidence. Our every attempt failed for one reason or another, usually because of the fact that we were flat scared to death of the blamed rooster. Our greatest help came from the most unexpected source — little brother Danny. Since Danny was 8 years younger than me and 11 years younger than Bobby, he wasn't allowed to play outside with us very much. I guess the grown-ups thought we might be a bad influence on him. They were probably right.

One summer day three pretty tough boys in the Safie neighborhood showed up on the front porch and announced that they had come to fight the meanest boy from Roberdel. So, the ever gracious Uncle Bobby invited them in. We went out back where Ma couldn't see us, and Bobby drew a ring in the sand. He put me inside the ring and told the boys to get in the ring one at the time, and the meanest boy in Roberdel would, "whip their butts as long as they wanted to fight." That entertained us for several hours.

While that was going on, Ma needed an egg and while she hated to send pretty little curly headed Danny to do the job, he was the only one in sight. He was happy to get this job which was usually reserved for the older kids. Off he went to his first encounter with Big Red. Danny had to reach as high as he could to unlatch the chicken lot gate, but he managed to reach just high enough to let himself in. He poked his head into the hen house and looked around. As his eyes adjusted to the dark, he could see an egg laying there in the nest. He grabbed it and started back outside when he saw Big Red's shadow, which made the rooster appear to be at least 4 feet tall. Since Danny had heard about Big Red's attacks on Bobby and me, he was scared out of his wits. Nonetheless, he headed for the chicken lot door, but Big Red was frightened too. He ran straight at Danny, knocking him to the ground and breaking the egg as well. Danny figured the rooster would surely kill him, and he screamed as loud as he could. Ma came running out the back door with her fly swatter in her hand. She ran the rooster away and surveyed the damage. Danny was filthy because a chicken lot is not a good place to fall down for several obvious reasons. He was skinned up a little bit, and he had Bobby and me as two ready-to-testify eye witnesses to his story of the unprovoked attack of the mad rooster. Ma took Danny inside to calm him down and to get the chicken droppings out of his hair.

The minute Granddad came into the house, we all started testifying about the awful attack on the innocent child. Ma called Granddad aside and told him flatly, "It's time for you to do something about that rooster!" Granddad walked calmly outside, went into the chicken lot and picked up Big Red, who was surely puzzled as to why his master didn't seem to appreciate him protecting the hens from the curly haired predator. Granddad went out on a grassy spot and snapped the head right off of Big Red. In 15 minutes he had cleaned the feathers off the rooster and delivered it inside to Ma. Later that evening we had fried chicken which Danny declares to this day was the best he's ever eaten.

Granddad's mark

I knew my Granddad had only attended school a couple of years, but I also knew that he was the wisest man that I had ever known. Therefore, when something happened that would expose his lack of formal education, I was always a little surprised.

For most of Granddad's life, he was paid partly in cash and partly in "dooky books." These books were actually coupon books which were only redeemable for goods at the company owned store, which carried clothing, household supplies and food. According to Granddad, they were okay to use at the company store, but if you tried to use them anywhere else, they weren't worth "dooky", therefore, the name.

Near the end of Granddad's textile career, the company started paying with checks. One day when I was visiting in their home, I saw a check lying on the kitchen table. It was face down with a salt shaker sitting on top to keep the gentle breeze which drifted through the open kitchen window from blowing it away. I was surprised to see an "X" on the spot where you expect someone to write their name. After a while I had a few minutes alone with Ma and I quietly asked her about the "X." She smiled gently and answered that the "X" was my Granddad's mark. As I often did, I had my other questions prepared before I had an answer to the first one. "What do you mean, his mark? Why didn't he just sign his name?" I was totally unprepared for her response. "Honey, your Granddad never learned to write his name." She patiently explained to me that Granddad had to begin working in the mill when he was just a child, and he wasn't able to do much schoolwork even though he attended a few years. I was shocked to say the least! I also was a little embarrassed both for him and for myself and most of all, I was mad as hell! He was much too smart to be using a mark for his signature.

I waited as patiently as teenage years would allow, but I was determined that my Granddad would learn to write his name. A few weeks later I began a little plan to let Granddad see me sitting around practicing my writing. Finally one day he said, "Geeboy, every time I see you, you're writing." That was just the opening I had been waiting for. I told him I had never been very good at handwriting, and my teachers had told me that I needed to practice. I asked him if he had ever practiced his handwriting much and he smiled and said, "I don't do much writing." I told him that it would make it more fun for me if he'd practice with me. He protested for a minute but I guess those memories of us working together in the garden and tending to the chickens were encouragement enough for him to sit down beside me on the bench at the kitchen table and pick up a pencil. I told him that we would just practice writing some letters first. He nodded his bald head, smiled and started making A's.

I suppose it was our third or fourth session when I suggested it was time to work on some words. We decided that the most important words we knew were our names. When I asked him if he would like to learn to write his name, he replied, "I don't guess I would mind too much." I asked him what his full name was, and he had a good chuckle before telling me — Willie Clarence McKinnon. I told him that was the ugliest name that I had ever heard, and he said that was why he never told anybody his middle name was Clarence. Since he had always told everybody his name was Willie C. McKinnon, I suggested we practice writing Willie C. McKinnon and that we shouldn't ever tell anybody his name was Clarence. He quickly agreed. After I wrote it out for him, he went to work and wrote Willie C. McKinnon over and over. I heaped praise on him and encouraged him to practice a few minutes every day. Later Ma would tell me about him sitting alone at the table, long past his usual 9:00 PM bedtime writing his name, and mine, over and over.

Then one day my big chance presented itself. I arranged to be there when his check came. Since Granddad never drove a car, I asked him if he would like me to take him and Ma to the grocery store, and he quickly took me up on the offer. When we finished buying the necessary items, we went together to the checkout counter. Of course, the clerk knew my grandparents well and when Granddad presented his check, she reminded him to put his mark on the back so they could cash it. Without a word passing between us, Granddad looked at me, with more than a little apprehension. In fact, he looked at Ma and me several times before he placed his hat on the counter, firmly grasped the pen and signed Willie C. McKinnon. Ma slipped her hand into his and gave him her most special smile. The clerk must have been shocked to say the least, but she said exactly the right thing, "Mr. McKinnon, you have the most beautiful handwriting I've ever seen." Granddad looked at me, smiled broadly and gave me a wink.

Beautiful, indeed!

No middle name

For some reason, the McGee family never seemed to care much about middle names. My father's name was simply, Sam McGee. His siblings included Roy, Cindy, Will, Millie, and Tanner, as well as a few others. They all had one given name so it's no surprise that when I was born, I was given the name of Jerry McGee, with no middle name.

The first time I noticed that almost everybody else had two given names was when we began first grade at the old Roberdel Elementary School. We were taught by Miss Mamie Monroe, who had taught most of our parents in earlier years. Sure enough the first day she called the roll, there was William Alvin Reynolds, William Ray Jameson, Margaret Diane Terry, Joanna Leigh Davidson, Mary Ann Little and on and on and on. However, when Miss Mamie got to my name, she simply called Jerry McGee. This did not go unnoticed by my new classmates, and more than once when I later visited in their homes, I would be introduced as "my friend, Jerry McGee, who doesn't have a middle name." I discussed this with my Daddy quite a few times, and he always said it was a real shame I only had one name, because he remembered during his time in the military when people had no middle name they would record them as Private John (no middle name) Smith. Somehow this made me think that I was different from everybody else, and I didn't find that particularly comforting.

Later when we got to Rockingham High School our teachers didn't know which name to call us, so they would call our entire name on the first day of each class. Those who had two given names simply told the teacher which name they preferred. The teacher would always ask me, "What is your middle name?" They never quite seemed to believe me when I told them I didn't have a middle name. This little exchange would annoy me greatly every year, but once classes got started I wouldn't think about the fact that I didn't have a middle name again for months.

Finally, on the first day of school during my senior year of high school, my homeroom teacher required us to fill out quite a few forms, all of which asked for a middle name. I went home that day and called the Richmond County Courthouse and asked how I could go about adding a middle name. They assured me that it was very simple. All I needed to do was come by the courthouse and tell them what name I needed to add, and they would take care of everything for me. They also told me that there would be a small charge for having a new birth certificate completed. I immediately found my mom and explained what I wanted to do, and she assured me she had no problem with me making such an addition. She then asked the obvious question, "What name are you going to add?" I had given the matter some thought in the past and I quickly responded, "Uncle Don McKinnon has always been one of my favorite relatives, and his middle name is Edward, so that's what I would like to add to my name." She chuckled at my reasoning, but gave her blessing. She wasn't the least bit surprised because she knew how much I loved Don, and she also was aware that he was the child who was the most like Granddad.

Realizing that the courthouse was open until 5 PM, I borrowed the family car and headed to town. After I was directed to the proper office, I requested that the middle name Edward be added to my birth certificate. Within minutes it was done and I plunked down 25 cents, which was the cost of having a new birth certificate completed. I had gone to town as simply Jerry McGee, and I was returning as Jerry Edward McGee. I thought, "Man this is great. I should have done it years earlier."

The next day my teacher called me to the front of the room and whispered to me, "I need to know your middle name in order for these forms to be complete. If your middle name is embarrassing or something you don't want the other students to hear, just whisper it to me." I leaned over and whispered, "Edward!" She looked very puzzled and said, "Jerry Edward McGee is a very nice name. Why didn't you just put your full name on the forms when you completed them yesterday?" She seemed a bit puzzled by my response, "I didn't have a middle name when I filled out the forms yesterday, but I do now." There was more than a little doubt in her look, but she put Edward in the place reserved for my middle name. Man, Jerry Edward McGee sure looked better than simply Jerry McGee.

That weekend I was laughing and telling Granddad about the conversation with my teacher. He had a really good chuckle as I described the look of disbelief she had given me. He thought that adding a middle name was the right thing to do, but he expressed one small regret. He thought I should have picked his middle name, Clarence. Sure, Granddad!

The Sitting & Talking Place

Leaving home

I owe my Uncle Bobby a lot. Besides teaching me about life, he also raised the bar in terms of education in our family. No one in our family had graduated from high school before Bobby came along. He graduated from Rohanen High School and enjoyed a very successful career with the United States Postal Service delivering mail in the Hamlet area. Rightfully, Granddad and Ma were very proud of him.

Our family lived in a part of Richmond County where young people went to work as soon as possible, some to help their families financially, and others simply to "get a head start on life" or to buy their first car and declare their independence. Very few finished their high school education. In fact, the only people we knew who had actually graduated from college were our medical doctors, school teachers and some of our ministers. They also were the most respected people we knew.

I'm not sure when it happened, but very early on, my Mama and Daddy began talking to me about going to college. I wasn't sure exactly what they meant, but since I loved school, it sounded all right to me. Somewhere along the line we all also figured out that going to college was a very expensive proposition. We had a lot of very bright kids in Roberdel and East Rockingham, but finances prevented most from reaching their full potential as far as education was concerned. I knew that some schools gave scholarships to athletes, but they seemed to be few in number. I also knew that no matter how much Mama and Daddy wanted me to go to college, there was simply no way they could afford to make a house payment, keep a good car, pay all the bills, provide for Danny and me and pay for college.

My family never let me lose the dream of going to college. I went out and found a couple of jobs, but the most important one was working at Archie's Red and White Grocery store. Archie and Helen Mudd were two of the hardest working people I've ever known, and they took great delight in helping youngsters who were honest and willing to work hard. They employed a lot of students along the way, including me, and later Danny. They were kind enough to let me work around my school and sports schedules and very often took me home after I finished work at 11 PM.

Granddad and Daddy were my financial advisers, and when I made $25 or $30 working part-time during the school years or $60 to

$75 working full-time in the summers and holidays, I would keep $3 or so for spending money and put the rest in my college account at the local savings and loan. I remember very well checking my bank account just before going off to school for my freshman year of college, and I had a little over $1,000 put away. That actually was quite an achievement since most of my deposits ranged from $5 to $20. It's hard to imagine anyone being any less prepared to go away to school than I was. Without anyone in our family, and practically no one I was acquainted with, who had gone to college, the learning curve was awfully steep.

There were some heartaches along the way. I was devastated when I didn't receive a prospective teacher loan, which I applied for in the spring of my senior year of high school. Also, I had to give up high school football so that I could work extra hours. I had to hitchhike everywhere because I couldn't afford a car, and one by one, schools decided they didn't need a 5' 9" third baseman who barely weighed 140 pounds. Fortunately, East Carolina College invited me to "walk on" and try out for the baseball team and I jumped at the chance.

As the time to go to college quickly approached, it began to dawn on me — "going away to college!" That meant leaving home and Mama and Daddy, Danny, Granddad, Ma and all of my supporters and encouragers. Quite frankly, I wasn't sure it was worth it. No more long talks with Granddad. No more home cooked meals prepared by Ma or Mama's loving hands. No more being one of the best baseball players. I would have to prove I was good enough to play college baseball or that I deserved to even be in college. Four years was a long time when you're only 17 and we really couldn't afford it anyway. Who was I kidding? If I stayed at home, I could get a job and help Mama and Daddy and get on with my life, for goodness sakes! Mama, Daddy and Granddad realized better than I that our relationships were about to change forever, but they knew that my attending college could be the most important thing in the history of our family. Every time I had second thoughts, they were right there providing encouragement, and I believe at this point, they were going to send me to college whether I wanted to go or not.

Granddad talked to me a lot during my high school days about the other grandchildren who were watching me. He told me of conversations between them when they quoted everything they had heard me say. Concerning college he said flatly, "You're going to college for

The Sitting & Talking Place

all of us. The mill has been good to us, but if you have a chance to be a school teacher, you have to do it." Still I knew my leaving home was hard for him, but I guess he had to get Bobby and me out of the way so that he could turn his attention to the other grandchildren who needed him as well.

When it came time for me to tell Ma and Granddad goodbye, I went by for lunch. Ma went all out and it was a wonderful meal. As I was giving Ma a goodbye hug, I noticed Granddad rattling around in his personal trunk, which had sat in the same spot in the kitchen for many years. He gave me a nod as he went out the back door, our unspoken signal that we needed to talk. I quickly followed him out into the shade, not knowing exactly what to say. We stood and talked for a minute before he reached into his pocket and pulled out four neatly folded five dollar bills. "Your Grandmother and I are proud of you and want to help you out a little bit," was all he said. Reluctantly, I took the money and thanked him and promised him that I would do my best. Once again, they were assuring me that I would never be alone.

The Sitting & Talking Place

The baseball fan

Once again, Granddad was right. During my college years the textile baseball leagues had a brief revival only to be replaced a few years later by slow pitch softball. However, the timing of the few years of textile baseball allowed me to play first for J. P. Stevens, and later for Ellerbe and Cordova during my summer breaks from college. This was baseball at its very best, and although it never regained its former popularity, those of us who participated had a great experience. It certainly wasn't like the old days of textile leagues, but it did assure that a pretty good baseball player could always get a summer job.

Between my freshman and sophomore years, J. P. Stevens hired me to do various odd jobs and finally to change shuttles. Although the shuttle changing job was physically demanding, playing for the company team meant you never had to worry about being assigned to the dreaded second shift, which ran from 4 PM to midnight. This was certainly not the right shift for a college boy, who tried to maintain some sort of social life. Sometimes, especially when we played a game out of town on a week night, you might find three or four baseball players in the parking lot changing from a baseball uniform and cleats to work clothes and sneakers before dashing inside, just before the 12:00 midnight whistle. Although there was no official company policy which allowed players to report late for work, the other workers would cover for us if we ran a little behind schedule.

Granddad never really admitted to paying much attention to the games, but he knew that we played our home games in the old Safie Ball Park, which we used to see from our "sitting and talking place" behind the little store at the end of Fifth Street. One night our team was engaged in quite a contest with the team from Norwood, who had beaten us at their ball park a few weeks before. I had one of those games you always dreamed of — five hits in five at bats. In fact, the last hit came in the bottom of the 10th inning with the score tied, the bases loaded and two outs. My sharp single between the short stop and second baseman drove in the winning run. We were all exhausted because the game had been delayed by a thunderstorm, and it was after 11 PM when it finally ended. We didn't have much time to celebrate as several of us had to rush to work.

The next day Granddad came out to Roberdel with Uncle Don to do a little fishing. We were sitting together with our bamboo poles when Granddad asked me how baseball was going. I told him about the past few games and then I gave him a recap of the previous night's game. I told him that as far as I could remember, that was the first time I'd ever had five hits in one game since my little league days. I also told him how important the game was for our team, since Norwood had beaten us earlier. Without realizing he was giving away his secret, he replied, "I was hoping you would get to bat in the last inning because I figured if you did, you'd get another hit."

I had no idea my Granddad had seen the game! I guess he was sitting in the dark on the wet grass at our "sitting and talking place." I wonder how many other games he watched.

The Sitting & Talking Place

Ma's last trip

Everyone in our family was delighted when Hannah Covington and I announced that we were getting married, but there was one problem — the wedding was planned for August 15th and I wasn't scheduled to graduate from college until that Thanksgiving. This created a lot of concern for Mama, Daddy and Granddad, but the thought of not going back to complete my degree was not a consideration for me. All I had to do was complete my student teaching and the long dreamt of college degree would be mine.

The wedding was beautiful, although the un-air conditioned Cartledge Creek Baptist Church had never been hotter. Hannah was radiant and both her mother and mine looked beautiful. Ma loved every minute of the ceremony and surrounding events, but Granddad, who never liked crowds or church very much, only made a token appearance, and after giving me a wink, headed back to Safie with Uncle Archie.

We went to Williamsburg, Virginia on our honeymoon, and we could not have been happier. After a few days, we called Hannah's mother and mine to thank them for such a beautiful wedding and to let them know we were safe. Mama was happy to hear from us, but had to share some bad news with us. Ma, like so many of our relatives before her, had suffered a stroke and was not doing very well. I asked how Granddad was doing, and she said, "He's scared to death and he's been asking when you would be home. I think he wants to talk with you as soon as possible."

Hannah and I had spoken of returning home a couple of days earlier than originally planned because I needed to prepare to go back to school (not to mention the fact that we were flat broke), so we headed back home the next day.

When we got to Roberdel, Mama seemed mighty glad to see us, and we briefly told her about our trip. She suggested that we have lunch and that I should go to see Ma and Granddad as quickly as possible. When I drove up to their house, nothing seemed any different, but when I walked into the family room where I had enjoyed the happiest and most carefree days of my life, I found a hospital bed where the Christmas tree was always placed. In it was my dear Grandmother with her beautiful silver hair. She was asleep and had an I.V. in her arm. Sitting in a chair with his hat in his hands was my Granddad. He looked so sad and frightened and for the first time I could ever remember, he looked very old and tired. His lips quivered as he said, "I'm glad you're home. I don't know what I'm going to do." It was almost like he thought everything would be better when I got there, but I wasn't sure what to do either.

I sat down beside Granddad, took his hand in mine and said, "Granddad, I think we need to pray." He nodded his head and said, "I've never gone to church much. I don't even know how to start praying." I quickly responded, "God hears everybody's prayers, Granddad. I'll start and you just join in any time you feel like it." We looked at each other and bowed our heads. I prayed as earnestly as I knew how. I asked for God's guidance as our family adjusted to Ma's illness and as we tried to do all we could to make her comfortable. I asked for God's healing hand to give Ma strength. When I had finished my prayer, I waited to see what Granddad would do. What he did was pray one of the most beautiful prayers I've ever heard. He spoke so lovingly of her dedication to her family and her church and of their mutual love for one another. He spoke of precious memories of their life together and of his commitment to caring for her in the days ahead, just as unselfishly as she had for so long cared for him. I've never been prouder of Granddad, and I told him so when we were finished.

Before I left I promised him that our family had always been close and that we would always be there for Ma and him. He nodded and tried to smile but the hurt was too deep.

I gave Ma a kiss on the forehead and she awoke briefly. When she realized I was crying, she smiled and told me not to cry because, "Will's going to take good care of me." I knew he would try, but I also knew our family's lives had just changed forever. Ma's last trip away from home had been to attend my wedding.

The graduate

When I graduated from college, there was great celebration, and, no doubt, a lot of relief that I had finished my work. The degree didn't come any too easily. I had to stay out of school one academic term because of a lack of money, and I usually had to work at least a couple of part-time jobs. I supplemented my finances by officiating intramural athletic events and eventually became the student director of the intramural program. Because of the involvement and support of a lot of people, I managed to graduate at the end of the fall term, 1965. A few days after I graduated, Mama told me that I should take my diploma and show it to Ma and Granddad. These were not good times for Granddad because Ma was very weak as a result of her stroke and had become completely bedridden. The roles had dramatically reversed, and Granddad was now responsible for feeding and caring for her with his only relief coming when other family members gave him a break.

Mama went with me, and we first showed the diploma to Ma. She smiled sweetly and said to me, "I've always known how smart you are. Now everybody else will know, too." She had always enjoyed the fact that when I came to stay with her when I was younger, I always seemed to have a stack of books from the bookmobile and read them cover to cover. "Go show it to Will," she insisted. "He's mighty proud of you."

Mama looked after Ma while Granddad and I headed to the store. The road was paved now and the store didn't seem so far away to me, but I suspect the walk now seemed much longer to Granddad. We got our soft drinks and without a word headed around to the back of the store. Sitting there in our favorite place, I opened up the tube and unrolled my East Carolina College diploma. He asked me to read it to him and I read every word. He asked about the signatures and who the people were who had signed it. I read the name of the Dean of the College and told him about his job at East Carolina. I read the names of the Chairman and Secretary of the Board of Trustees and discussed what the Trustees did, then I read him the name of Dr. Leo Jenkins, the President of the University. I told him of my admiration for Dr. Jenkins because he had done so much for East Carolina and its students. Granddad seemed to be very excited about my graduation and told me that he hoped all of the other grandchildren would go to college now that I had made it through.

The Sitting & Talking Place

Then he asked a question that really took me by surprise. He wanted to know if he could take my diploma to the mill one day. I was dumbfounded because I never imagined this might happen. He went on to tell me how he often told his friends and co-workers that I was going to college so that I could teach school. He said that he was proud of me, but that he didn't tell them about me going to college to be bragging. He was trying to show them that if I could go to college, so could their children and grandchildren. He told them how hard I worked after school, during the summer and holidays and how I saved my money. He wanted them to know that it wasn't easy, but that it was possible and that they needed to keep their children in school as long as possible.

He told me how some of "the little half-assed supervisors" at the mill laughed and told him that I would never make it in college, and that I would wind up back in the mill before long. They told Granddad more than once that, "You can't make somebody out of nobody." He also told me about how the people who swept the floors, the weavers and shuttle changers always asked how I was doing and told him to let me know they were pulling for me. Of course, I had never known about any of this, and Granddad knew that it was probably best I didn't. I was under enough pressure as it was, and I sure didn't need to know that there were some people hoping that I would fail.

I left my diploma with Granddad so that he could show it to his friends and co-workers as proof that a boy from the mill hill could, indeed, graduate from college when he had a family behind him. I wish I could have heard him explaining to them who the Dean and the President were and what their jobs were at East Carolina.

I suspect Granddad would be pleased to know that I would graduate from college two more times and that I would become President of Wingate University, where I would be the one to sign the diplomas.

Where to serve?

Will & Betty McKinnon had seven children, four sons and three daughters. As often was the case during their days, the children were born over a period spanning nearly 20 years. This certainly made for a lively household and provided plenty of help to both parents as they dutifully tended to their family responsibilities.

The disadvantage to having boys during those years was the ever present threat of wars and conflicts around the world which often called young men into military service. Uncle Archie McKinnon was quick to enlist in the U. S. Navy during World War II and served with distinction. Fortunately, he saw only limited combat duty, but for parents who seldom left Richmond County, North Carolina, the war in the Pacific was terribly frightening. Correspondence was difficult in the 1940s so a family had to depend on its strong belief in their country, as well as their faith, to see them through such difficult and lonely times. The infrequent letters from servicemen were read over and over and shared with relatives and neighbors. Unfortunately, the news of combat injuries and deaths were far too numerous and left most families praying for the best while preparing for the worst.

Even though wars are always traumatic for everyone involved, Uncle Archie took full advantage of his opportunity to see the world, made many close personal friends and brought home a lifetime of memories. Later he and I would spend many hours fishing together while he told me about places he had been, people he had met and a lot of stories I couldn't share with my Mother. To a large degree he provided my introduction to a larger world outside of my personal world, which consisted of Roberdel and East Rockingham.

The Korean Conflict didn't call any of the McKinnon boys into service, but provided my grandparents with two son-in-laws. Both of the twins, Loyce and Joyce, met and married young men who were serving in the U. S. Army at Fort Bragg at this time. Loyce married Charles Reppond and later moved to Tennessee, and Joyce married Don Phillips from the state of Washington, and they moved to Arizona. Unfortunately, the distances involved kept them from visiting as often as the family would have liked and their children, regrettably, enjoyed very little contact with the other members of the family.

The Vietnam War provided a startling and unwelcomed upset in the McKinnon family because Uncle Bobby and I were both at draft age during this time. Fortunately, for me, I enjoyed a student deferment classification because I was enrolled in college. However, Bobby was drafted, sent to basic training and immediately dispatched to Vietnam, a place we all had trouble finding on a map. This war stood in stark contrast to World War II, which was clearly fought to defend America against its world enemies. No one seemed to quite understand why our young men and women should go fight a war on behalf of people who seemed so unappreciative of our sacrifices and unwilling to fight for themselves. But Bobby went as ordered and did his patriotic duty, just as hundreds of thousands of other young Americans. Although no military duty is without danger during the time of war, he was fortunately assigned to a supply unit a good distance from the front lines, and he served well, but without direct combat experience.

For aging parents, front lines or not, Vietnam was Vietnam and they predictably were disappointed that their youngest son was called to military duty and heartbroken when he was sent to this strange country to fight in such an unusual war. Granddad and I had quite a few long talks about the Vietnam War and he, no doubt, knew I was as frightened for Bobby as he was. Very often when we were together he would ask me if I thought Bob would be okay. Although I was very concerned, I would always be positive and assure him that Bobby would be fine. I told him that if Bobby was able to take on Big Red, the rooster, that he could certainly handle himself in dealing with the Viet Cong.

More than once Granddad and I talked about how long the war might last and wondered together if it would still be going on after I finished college. Although we both hoped otherwise, it appeared that this war would last a long, long time. Sadly, our observations were correct. By this time it had become obvious to everyone, except President Johnson, Congress and our military leaders, that we needed to get our troops home and declare this debacle over, but our men and women were left there and continued to serve valiantly. After my college days ended and Hannah and I were married, our family faced together the reality that I would soon be called to serve in the military.

Of course, some members of the family felt I should happily serve if called on, but others felt strongly that I should find an alternative if at all possible. Of course, with a new wife and job, I was ready to get on with my life rather than going away to fight for a cause most Americans no longer believed in. I tried to talk to as many reasonable people as I could, but emotions ran very high on this sensitive issue. As usual, my best advice came from Granddad. He felt our family had contributed generously to every military conflict our country had been involved in and that, "my family needed me more than Vietnam did." I told him flatly that I sure didn't want to, "go get killed at the tail end of a war I didn't understand," but that I, "was no better than Uncle Bobby and my friends who had done their military duty." I felt I could get a commission as a Second Lieutenant and perhaps fly helicopters or serve in an intelligence unit. His reply was, "or you could stay here and be a husband, son and grandson and maybe a daddy." I was taken back by his directness and reminded him again that our family had always served when called on and that I had to do what was right. Without hesitation he told me that I was, "smart enough to figure out something if I put my mind to it." He said, "I don't know much about this Vietnam mess, but Betty and I don't want both you and Bobby over there at the same time."

A few days later I contacted a long time family friend, Sgt. Erskine Bostick who was in charge of the local National Guard unit. Someone was obviously looking out for me and my family because Sgt. Bostick said the guard was only taking new members who had previous military service UNLESS I would take and pass a test which would make me eligible for Officers Training School. I agreed to take the test immediately, passed easily and was sworn into the North Carolina National Guard that same day. This would require a six year commitment, including six months in active duty. But it also provided exactly what I was looking for — a way to serve my country and to provide the leadership for my family that Granddad had reminded me I owed them.

Thankfully, Bobby soon returned home safely to a loving wife, Patricia, and later fathered a son, Brian, and a daughter, Jill. Unfortunately, a number of our friends and neighbors were killed or badly wounded in Vietnam in a war we still don't fully understand.

The Sitting & Talking Place

The enemy

After my college graduation I accepted a position in industrial engineering with Klopman Mills in Cordova, which is just a few miles south of Rockingham. I had planned to be a school teacher, but when I began interviewing, I discovered that those jobs didn't pay very well and they only provided nine months employment each year. I was offered a teaching position in another county which would have required us to relocate, but neither Hannah nor I found that to be very attractive. She had a job at the local library, which she seemed to enjoy, and both our families were in Rockingham, so I accepted the industrial engineering position with the understanding that I would be considered for a position in the personnel office when an opening occurred. This textile position paid the bills, but it was too confining for me to consider it a long term position. Of course, the personnel position never happened.

I didn't realize it immediately, but by accepting a job in textile management I had disappointed a lot of my high school friends and some members of my own family. I soon found out that the industrial engineering department was the most disliked part of the textile management operation. When industrial engineering went into a department to do a study of a particular job, we usually increased production demands. The workers, many of whom I had grown up with or was remotely related to, thought they were already producing all they could. Even when I did a study or two which seemed to help the workers by moving equipment to locations which didn't demand such strenuous labor or suggested adding additional workers to aid production, most of those affected assumed we had some unpopular motive in mind.

Finally, one Sunday when our extended family got together for lunch, my Uncle Hayden put it very bluntly, "When we finally got somebody to graduate from college, we sure didn't expect you to come back and work in the mill. If my children are lucky enough to get a college education, I guarantee I'll never let them do what you did." I was totally taken by surprise but before I could respond he added, "You disappointed all of us but especially your Grandfather. He thought you were going to teach school." Oh, no, I thought. As far as my family was concerned, I had become the enemy.

As soon as I could recover, I knew what I had to do. I got Granddad's attention and nodded to him to go outside with me. We walked out to the garden and I looked at him and said, "Granddad, I'm sorry if I've disappointed you and the rest of our family. I never intended to work in the mill very long, but I've got my military duty coming up and when I get back, I'm going to try to get a job in education." His sad eyes lit up a little and he replied simply, "That would make your Grandmother and me very happy." And, that's what I did!

The Sitting & Talking Place

Old and alone

I was alone when the telephone rang in the office I shared with two co-workers at Klopman Mills. It was my mother. Her voice was unusually strained as she told me directly, "Honey, I hate to call you at work, but your Grandmother died a little while ago. You need to come as soon as you can." I said, "I will be right there, mama. I love you very much." With a breaking voice, she replied simply, "I know. I love you, too."

Although Ma had grown weaker each day following her stroke, I had never lost a close relative since I had become old enough to know what death meant. I was stunned, and when one of my co-workers walked in, he sensed something was wrong. I told him quickly that my Grandmother had just died and that my family needed me more than Klopman did right now. I grabbed my jacket and headed for Safie.

By the time I arrived, Mama and Daddy and most of my uncles and their wives were already there. I walked quickly into the kitchen which was filled with family, friends and neighbors. Still, it sure seemed empty without Ma. I asked where Granddad was and Mama pointed out back. I went out the back door and predictably found him feeding his chickens. I went into the chicken lot, grabbed a handful of feed and joined him in this chore, which we had done together dozens of times. We didn't speak for a while because he seldom had anything to say, and I didn't know what to say. After we used all the feed we had with us, I dusted off my hands and looked him straight in the eye and said, "Granddad, all you have ever asked of me was for me to do my best. We all know you did your best for Ma and that's all you could do. I love you. Everything will be all right." He quietly replied, "I know you love me, son, but everything won't be all right. Betty meant everything to me. I don't know what I'll do without her."

Those dear neighbors hadn't forgotten the vegetables Granddad had delivered to them over the years. He had been a wonderful neighbor and this was their chance to pay him back. They filled the kitchen table, the refrigerator, and the stove with an unbelievable amount of food. Grandmother loved flowers and they literally piled into the house and the funeral home. She would have been so pleased.

The Sitting & Talking Place

We all had jobs to do but I think Hannah, Mama and Uncle Archie drew the toughest assignment of all. They took Granddad to the funeral home to select a coffin and make funeral arrangements, then they accompanied him to town to buy Ma a new dress for the funeral. Ma was always a beautiful woman who loved pretty clothes. Since she had been bedridden for almost a year and a half, it was important to Granddad that she have something new and pretty to wear. According to Hannah, they went to Ma's favorite downtown store, Belk's. A long time family friend who worked in the store showed them every dress she had to offer. They tried to encourage Granddad to buy a reasonably priced dress, but he kept insisting that he wanted to buy the nicest dress in the store. When they finished shopping, Granddad had selected the prettiest and most expensive dress in the shop. Archie offered to pay for the dress, but Granddad would have no part of it. As he reached for his wallet, he said, "This is the last dress I can buy for Betty, and I want it to be a nice one and it doesn't matter what it costs."

Ma looked beautiful in the dress, the church was filled with friends, family and flowers. She was buried at Green Lake Cemetery, which is located about equal distance between her favorite places — Ledbetter and Roberdel. She was placed alongside her beloved Curries and Lovins. After the funeral, we all went back to our house in Roberdel while the funeral director finished his work. Then we returned to the cemetery just before dark. Granddad and I stood silently among the beautiful flowers. After a while he looked at me and said, "It's time to go home. I've got some things to do." As we walked to the car, his broken heart wouldn't allow him to come up with a smile, but he did manage to give me a wink. I've never loved him more than I did at that moment.

The birthday boys

One of the many things Granddad and I shared was our birthdays. Well, not exactly, but close enough. Granddad's birthday was November 3rd and mine was November 4th. Later Hannah and I had a son, Ryan, who also "shared" that birthday, November 2. Birthdays were never a big deal in our family once you reached the age of 16. After that you might get a card or two, but nobody seemed to be very excited about being a year older. Granddad always said after a person turned 16 and got a driving license, the next important birthday was 65 when you could retire from work.

After Granddad was widowed, though, my mother did take advantage of our shared birthdays and made them really special occasions. She would bill the day as a birthday dinner for Granddad and me and invite everybody in the family to come. Sometimes only a few dropped by, but on other occasions we'd have a houseful. She would prepare a wonderful meal and bake a birthday cake with lots of candles. Granddad would fuss a little bit, but he always showed up with a big old smile on his face. He would stand back and make me blow out the candles and try to act like he was just there to celebrate my birthday. But when everybody sang Happy Birthday to the two of us, he always seemed to enjoy it a lot. He opened every present very carefully and with great anticipation and laughed more on this day than any other day of the year. The longest and hardest I have ever seen Granddad laugh was one year when someone got our presents mixed up and put his name on mine and my name on his. He got a new hairbrush that was meant for me — which was pretty funny because he had been bald for 40 years. Then I opened three pairs of size 38 boxer shorts which was supposed to be for him because I wore size 30 jockey shorts.

As the big day ended he would always tell Mama that she shouldn't go to all that trouble again the next year. Fortunately, she didn't listen to him, and the next year there we were again celebrating birthdays the first week of November.

When it came time to take him home following these big cele-brations, we usually stopped by the cemetery to visit Ma's grave for a few minutes. At the end of the day I never wanted to leave, because I always hated to leave him alone, and because I knew that he was run-ning out of birthdays. I couldn't imagine life without my Granddad.

The Sitting & Talking Place

Wrestling comes to East Rockingham

After Ma's death, Granddad spent a lot of time watching television. He didn't particularly care for the world news. His world was East Rockingham, North Carolina. He never really got into sports unless I was playing, with one exception – he really, really liked wrestling. The main problem was that his hearing had gotten pretty bad due to his advancing age and more than 50 years of listening to textile machinery at work. Several neighbors complained about the volume of his television set, but he paid little attention to any of them. Many times I remember pulling up in front of his house, and having his television drown out the sound of my car engine and radio.

He had moved to a small house near Rohanen High School, and one day when I was visiting, he had big news. Wrestling was coming live to the Rohanen High School gym, just a short distance from his front door. I asked if he'd like to go with me to the great performance. His sad eyes lit up quickly, and he gave me that famous Willie C. McKinnon smile. I explained that I had to work on the day of the main event, but assured him I would get tickets and that although I might be a little late, we would definitely go to the wrestling match.

The Hamlet Jaycees were sponsoring the evening of wrestling to raise money to support their work in the community. A quick call to my friend, and Jaycee President David Davenport, took care of the tickets. I told David I might be running a little late, so I asked him to reserve two front row tickets and a good parking space. He was glad to oblige and told me that he couldn't imagine me at a wrestling match, much less on the front row.

It was truly a night to remember. I got to Granddad's at 7:20 PM – 10 minutes before the match started. He was waiting on the porch with his hat on and ready to go. We drove up the street and quickly found our prized parking space, just as promised. David met us at the door with our tickets, and we slid into our front row seats just as the first battlers were being introduced. Granddad thought there was a mistake, but I assured him that we had reserved the best seats in the house.

We had a great time. We saw Billy Two Rivers win his match against a Japanese fighter by using his famous tomahawk chop. We saw two midget wrestlers go at it for a while before one finally put the sleeper hold on the other fighter, who was quickly counted out. We even saw two bald headed Russians apparently win their match before they were rightfully disqualified for using a foreign object to knock the daylights out of their opponents. In fact, Granddad saw the foreign object before the referee, and his screaming actually alerted the referee to the cheating Russians and caused their disqualification. I was a little worried the Russians might be waiting for us outside after the match, but fortunately, they were not. I guess they had to get back to Moscow.

The main event started at nearly 10:00 PM. I had seldom seen Granddad awake past 9:30, but he wasn't sleepy tonight. The two greatest fighters in the world at that time were George Becker and Johnny Weaver. They were the international world champion tag team and they were so close they were sweating on Granddad and me. Weaver and Becker won the first fall easily, but the villains won the second fall by double teaming George Becker when the referee wasn't looking. The third and final fall took a while and it looked like the world championship might be lost. But somehow Johnny Weaver, after being beaten for a full 10 minutes, found enough strength to throw his opponent out of the ring and right into Granddad's lap. At first Granddad seemed startled and confused but he recovered quickly and pushed the villain to the floor. George Becker ran around the out-side of the ring and jerked the villain away from Granddad and tossed him back into the ring where his partner, Johnny Weaver, quickly pinned him. The championship had been defended! The popular champions, Becker and Weaver paraded around the ring with their championship belts held high over their heads. They came to our side of the ring and pointed to Granddad and motioned for him to stand up. After I urged him to take a bow, he stood to the thunderous applause of everyone in the audience. There he was, my Granddad, the wrestling fan, chuckling and enjoying the moment.

After dropping Granddad off at his place, I couldn't wait to get home to call my mother and share the news. It took a while to get my call through, and when I did, she laughed and said, "Everybody in East Rockingham has already called and your Granddad has called twice himself." Before that night, I wasn't sure he could even dial the tele-phone.

The beginning of the end

Perhaps it was 50 years of breathing the unhealthy air in the various cardrooms in the mills of Roberdel and East Rockingham. Maybe it was all those years of steadily smoking Lucky Strikes (we didn't know then about the health hazards associated with cigarettes). It could have been the loneliness and the heartache of losing his beloved Betty. More than likely it was a combination of all these things. Whatever the reason, Granddad began to cough a lot. It was difficult to see him suffer one health problem after another because he had always seemed so strong and invincible.

Mama and my uncles, Hayden, Archie, Don and Bob, spent a lot of their time looking after Granddad, and they became increasingly concerned about his health. Rather than getting better, it seemed his health worsened, and he eventually had to be hospitalized. At that time Richmond Memorial Hospital wasn't much more than a first aid station and baby birthing center. When someone had a difficult to diagnose problem, they were routinely referred to Moore Memorial Hospital in Pinehurst. This was, and still is, a very fine hospital with many well-trained physicians and the very best equipment and facilities. Granddad was taken to Moore Memorial right away, but not much was known about Brown Lung and other breathing problems in those days. Things didn't look good at all.

After he was there a few days Mama told me that she thought it might lift his spirits if I'd travel the 35 miles or so to see him. That Saturday I drove up to Pinehurst, and I was shocked to see him hooked up to several machines. When he saw me, his eyes lit up and he quickly motioned for me to come closer. He was obviously trying to tell me to look down his throat. Although he could only talk in a whisper, there was no doubt he was glad I was there. I talked to the nurse about his throat, and she promised to tell the doctor when he came by later.

For a while we just sat. It was pretty much like old times. I talked and he listened. He'd been enjoying getting to know our three year old son, Ryan, before he started feeling so bad, and he had seen our new son, Sam, a few times since his birth a few weeks earlier. Every now and then, when I was talking about the boys, he would tap my arm and whisper, "You used to be just like that." Or, "They sound just like you and Bob."

After a good long visit I told him I'd better get home and rescue Hannah from the boys. He got a pretty good chuckle from that. Then he closed his eyes and appeared to be going to sleep.

The next day I saw Uncle Archie at Mama's, and he was thrilled at the improvement in Granddad's condition when he had visited earlier in the day. He said that after the nurse told the doctor about Granddad's complaint about his throat, the doctor found a growth-like obstruction. After it was removed, his breathing was dramatically improved, and his voice was much stronger. We all became hopeful but soon discovered that a tired 76 year old body doesn't bounce back very quickly. But this was Willie C. McKinnon, a man who had spent a lifetime beating the odds. I prayed he could do it again.

Going to be with Betty

When I arrived at Moore Memorial Hospital, it was obvious this visit was different from the earlier ones. Before I entered Granddad's room I could hear his labored breathing. As I approached his bed, his eyes were closed, but he opened them weakly as I pulled up a chair. I sat for a while not knowing what to say or do, but absolutely sure that I was where I needed to be.

His face was flushed so I placed my hand on his head to check for a fever. He opened his eyes, looked at me and smiled faintly. He wasn't trying to speak, but he was barely moving the fingers on his left hand. Knowing how it used to make me feel better when he held my hand, I took his hand in mine, and he nodded his head slightly and went back to sleep. After I had sat there holding his hand for a while, he awakened and I could tell he was trying to tell me something, but it was very difficult to make words out of his whispers. Finally, I asked him if he was talking about Ma and his eyes answered, "Yes." I finally could understand the words, "Betty, . . . died . . . tomorrow." He was trying to remind me that Ma had died on December 6, and that tomorrow was the anniversary of her death. Then he whispered, "flowers." I finally had the message that he wanted flowers put on his beloved Betty's grave tomorrow. I quickly assured him that I would take care of it. Again he smiled. I thought to myself, "How true his love for Ma must be! Here he is near death himself, and all he can think about is buying her flowers."

I knew it was long past the time I should go but I didn't want this visit to end, so I just sat there holding the hand of the wisest and most important man in my life. He had taught me how to be a man and prepared me for life in a world he would not have understood.

Finally, I simply had to go home. Waiting for me were my wife, who despite my imperfections, loved me with all her heart – just as Ma had loved Granddad – and two small sons, who were depending on me to teach them about life – just as Granddad had taught Bobby and me. I hoped Granddad would open his eyes because I suspected he had been awake for a while, but I knew, as he did, that if he didn't watch me leave, it would be easier for both of us. I gently released his hand, kissed him on the forehead and said, "Granddad I love you with all of my heart." Then I realized he was crying . . . then I realized I was, too.

Willie Clarence McKinnon died the next day, December 6, 1973, exactly seven years following the death of his beloved wife, Elizabeth Currie McKinnon. He lies beside her at Green Lake Cemetery, about halfway between Roberdel and Ledbetter and only a few minutes from East Rockingham. He patiently waits for me there. We have much to talk about.